Y0-BWC-753

ACTON ON HISTORY

By the same author

RUSSIA AND THE WEIMAR REPUBLIC

LIONEL KOCHAN

ACTON ON HISTORY

ANDRE DEUTSCH

First published 1954 by
ANDRE DEUTSCH LIMITED
12 Thayer Street, Manchester Square
London W1

Printed in Great Britain by
TONBRIDGE PRINTERS LTD
Tonbridge Kent

As before, to Winkle

ACKNOWLEDGEMENTS

I am indebted to the Editors of *The Cambridge Journal* and *The Contemporary Review* for kind permission to reprint portions of articles that originally appeared in their pages.

L. K.

CONTENTS

Note on Method

'THE greatest men ...' runs one of Acton's notes, 'you can quote for everything.' He instances Shakespeare, Leibniz and Burke[1]. Without in any way prejudging Acton's intellectual stature, this is an assertion that applies very much to its author. It is hardly necessary to place Acton in the same company as, for example, Leibniz to become aware that Acton, too, can be 'quoted for almost everything'. Partial readings of Acton abound, to an extent that is sometimes contradictory. To Professor Morgenthau he represents one of 'the great non-liberal thinkers in the liberal age'[2]. Elsewhere, however, Acton has been cogently treated as part and parcel of the same liberal age[3]. Who is in the right? Was Acton a liberal or not? This is but one example of the divergent and seemingly irreconcilable Actons that co-exist. It might be complemented by another that sees in him a man of pitiless consistency, who regularly rode his formulae to death – yet whose work suffered from a fundamental inconsistency.

The present study does not claim to resolve these contradictions, although it is hoped to show that they are not as irreconcilable as might appear. If there are without doubt many sides to Acton, there is in the last resort only one Acton. The present aim is to examine as thoroughly as the evidence permits one side of this one Acton. The title – *Acton on History* – has been chosen in order to suggest that concern is with his presuppositions, with the attitude preceding his consideration of any historical question, if the two may somewhat artificially be separated. (The sketch of Acton's life and historical background in the Introduction is simply intended to put the reader in the picture.) This excludes from interest, *for their own sake*, Acton's views of any specific historical period, or historian, philosopher or politician. Rather, views of this kind are where necessary abstracted from their subject-matter and set in the more general framework of Acton's historical attitude.

In the elucidation of this attitude the notes, now located at the University Library, Cambridge, that Acton compiled for his unwritten life's work – *The History of Liberty* – enjoy a special position[4]. Contained in some five hundred boxes and notebooks, they mostly consist of innumerable extracts, each on a separate slip of paper, and usually unclassified, from authors to whom he intended to refer in some way, not always specified or apparent. Embodied amongst these extracts is an occasional slip of paper or a page of a notebook bearing a note by Acton himself. These notes are very rarely dated and all that can be said with certainty is that they belong to the period 1875-1900. However, as they do not offer any evidence of 'layers' of thought there is no reason, barring one or two early notebooks (dated as such) why they should not be treated *en bloc*, even though some of the notes may precede others by as much as a quarter of a century.

The notes, as distinct from the quotations, have two other aspects that must be mentioned. They are, in the first place, frequently more abstract than Acton's other writings, in the sense that they deal with general questions of the historical attitude and not so much with particular aspects of history or historians. In the second place, the notes, excluding of course the quoted extracts, are the repository of Acton's genuine sentiments in a way that was not always the case with his published works or letters. (The reason why this distinction should have existed, together with illustrative examples, is adduced below in the Introduction.) Therefore, other things being equal, the argument of the notes is here preferred to that of the published reviews, articles, letters, lectures, etc. This must not of course be taken to mean that the published works can at all be neglected. But it does mean that they must be weighed against what has remained unpublished and that when a choice has to be made the latter is to be preferred as the more authentic expression.

As this procedure makes clear, the present study is an attempt to *reconstruct* something that exists in an unfinished state. This is obviously a hazardous proceeding. There is no doubt that Acton did concern himself with working out a historical attitude. There is equally little doubt that, formally speaking, he did not produce a system though he sometimes wrote as though he had. He produced instead a series of notes couched in the most summary form. A reconstruction therefore is exposed to the ever-present danger of seeing a pattern where none exists or a meaning quite different from that intended. In these circumstances the nature of the material has dictated the nature of its presentation. Where the choice lies, as it does here, between a possible understatement and a no less possible overstatement of Acton's views, it has been deemed preferable to choose the former. Generally speaking, faults of omission have been preferred to faults of commission.

Certain liberties have been taken in the punctuation and arrangement of Acton's notes. Despite all the reflection and reading that lay behind them, they bear every trace of having been penned in an immense hurry, and are seldom punctuated except by dashes. Where obscurity might result, this omission has been remedied in the interests of clarity. For the same reason, the layout of the notes has been standardised. In the original, they are almost as often written vertically as horizontally, and sometimes even diagonally. Of course, where a word or phrase has been omitted in a quotation from the notes, this is indicated in the usual way by a series of dots. Conversely, a bracketed word or phrase is indicative of an addition, again made for the sake of clarity. Lastly, Acton's very frequent abbreviations have been spelt out in full, in preference to wearying the reader with the constant necessity to consult a key.

Introduction

I: A SKETCH OF ACTON'S LIFE

SOME forty years ago the late H. A. L. Fisher wrote of Lord Acton that 'though many men of his time were more famous, few left behind them a larger legacy of unsatisfied curiosity'[1]. Fisher, who had at one time studied under Acton, was not the only one of Acton's circle of friends and acquaintances to point to his obscure legacy. It was likewise noted by many who had known Acton over a longer period and more closely than had Fisher. To such people for example, as Gladstone, Viscount Morley, Bishop Creighton, Viscount Bryce and Lady Blennerhassett, Acton represented an enigma, bewildering if not impenetrable. Acton himself remarked, in a jocular, unhistorical mood: 'No secret lasts longer than twenty-seven years'[2]. In his own case this has shown itself to be an optimistic underestimate. Despite the increased attention given of late to Acton, it cannot be said that he has as yet been laid bare. Nor is this situation likely to alter until more material is made available. In the meantime all that can profitably be attempted is to clothe with some semblance of flesh the bare biographical bones.

John Emerich Edward Dalberg-Acton was born at Naples in the Palazzo Acton in January, 1834. His father was English, the descendant of a family whose connection with its estate at Aldenham in Shropshire could be traced back to the fourteenth century. Gibbon, who belonged to the same stock, described it as 'that ancient and loyal family of Shropshire baronets'. In the late seventeenth and early eighteenth century, Gibbon added, it consisted of 'seven brothers, all of gigantic stature; one of whom, a pigmy of six feet two inches, confessed himself the last and the least of the seven; adding, in the true spirit of party, that such men were not born since the Revolution'. Acton's great-grandfather, a doctor, attended Gibbon's father during the latter's tour of France, but then, in Gibbon's words 'the physician himself was attacked by the malady of love: he married his mistress, renounced his country and religion, settled at Besançon, and became the father of three sons'[3].

The eldest of these three sons – General Sir John Acton, as he afterwards became – was the historian's grandfather. The General seems to have been no less adventurous than his father. He crowned a career in the service of the Queen of Naples by becoming the Queen's Prime Minister. His activity in this role included a period as head of a reign of terror in Palermo during the Napoleonic Wars. By a special dispensation of the Pope, Sir John married his own niece and it was from this unhealthy union that Acton's father, Sir Richard Ferdinand Acton, was born. Aged thirty-five, he died at Paris in 1837.

Acton's mother was a Dalberg, of the South German Catholic aristocracy. His maternal grandfather, Reichsfreiherr Wolfgang Heribert von Dalberg was known for his liberal sympathies. He had, for example, protected Schiller on the latter's flight from Stuttgart; and as *Intendant* of the Mannheimer Theater at Baden had produced the dramatist's first play *Die Räuber* in 1782. The Dalberg estates lay at Herrnsheim in the Rhineland. Napoleon conferred a dukedom on the Dalberg's, and in 1810 Acton's grandfather accordingly forsook Baden for service under the French. On the Bourbon restoration in 1814, he was appointed by Louis XVIII to represent, together with Talleyrand, French interests at the Congress of Vienna.

Three years after the premature death of her husband,

Acton's mother, a young widow of twenty-three, married *en secondes noces* Lord Leveson, who later became the second Earl Granville and liberal Foreign Minister under Lord John Russell and Gladstone. The Catholic ceremony took place at the Spanish Chapel in London and the Protestant at Devonshire House, Piccadilly.

Acton's Catholic upbringing did not suffer from his mother's second marriage to a Protestant. In 1843 at the age of nine he began to attend Oscott College, then directed by the future Cardinal Wiseman. At a time when it first becomes possible to say something of Acton's character, it is clear that he was extremely precocious and ambitious. Few though the letters are, that survive his schooldays, they all speak naïvely of great intellectual ambitions and capacity. A year after his entry to Oscott he wrote to his mother: 'I am a perfect linguist, knowing perfectly – that is, so as to be able to speak them – English, French, German, and can almost speak Latin. I can speak a few words of Chinese, Greek, Italian, Spanish and Irish. I also know Chemistry, Astronomy, Mechanics, and many other sciences, but do not know botany.' Not surprisingly, the ten-year-old boy signs this letter – 'Caesar Agamemnon John Dalberg Acton'[4]. Some three years later Acton writes that he is devoting himself to poetry and is reading 'divine Pope' as well as Maria Edgeworth, Johnson, Scott, Dante, Tasso and Thompson. He reads too, the classics, French and German historians, and 'a German book that contains every alphabet of the East and West, this not without the help of a dictionary'[5]. Before long Acton found that his intellectual demands could no longer be satisfied by the resources available at Oscott. 'It is impossible', he wrote to his mother, 'to fulfil any further in Oscott my duties to God, to you and to myself in the way that I should. The institution is very good for most young people but not for me. My strongest passion – the desire to make a name for myself – can, I am quite sure, only be satisfied if I develop through my studies the gifts that heaven has conferred on me, and here I do not find competition'[6].

When Acton left Oscott he spent some time at Edinburgh, living as a private pupil with Dr Logan, a former Vice-President of the school. The aim was to improve his knowledge of Greek. It was his hope that he would be able to complete his education at Cambridge. But three Colleges rejected him, evidently on account of his religion. It was then decided that the sixteen-year-old boy would live and study with Professor Ignaz von Döllinger of Munich University where he would also be able to follow selected courses of lectures. In 1850 Acton arrived at Munich. Döllinger was then aged fifty-one and stood at the height of his fame as the foremost Catholic scholar in Germany. He wrote and lectured on ecclesiastical history and theology. In this atmosphere, created by a man much older than himself, Acton was able to find the competition and stimulation that he so ardently desired. It was in this period of his later teens that he laid the basis of his vast scholarship. A letter written shortly after arrival at Munich gives some idea of the initial scope of Acton's studies: 'I breakfast at 8 – then two hours of German – an hour to Plutarch, and an hour to Tacitus. This proportion was recommended by the Professor (*i.e.* Döllinger). We dine a little before 2 – I see him then for the first time in the day. At 3 my German master comes. From 4 till 7 I am out – I read modern history for an hour – having had an hour's ancient history just before dinner. I have some tea at 8 and study English literature and composition till 10 – when the curtain falls'[7]. Among the courses that Acton later followed at the University were economics, philosophy, ecclesiastical and medieval history, and theology.

In all this, Döllinger played the part of a quasi-omniscient supervisor. Many years afterwards Acton suffered deep disillusion with Döllinger, but at this time he termed him 'one of the greatest scholars'[8]; and even later, Döllinger, of all the scholars whom Acton came to know, was the only one to whom his notes refer simply as 'the Professor' or 'my Professor'. Döllinger, in fact, became for Acton a sort of father-figure. His own father had died before the son could know him. With Granville, his stepfather, he could have little in common. If Acton was more at home in the world of books, Granville was more at home in the book of the world. 'The Professor', on the other hand, represented for the youthful scholar all his own intellectual ideals and strivings. He became the symbol of the disinterested search for truth.

This intellectual harmony developed at a more personal level on the journeys that Döllinger and his pupil undertook during the University vacations. Together they visited most parts of Germany, as well as Italy, France and Bohemia. Acton also visited the United States (at the age of nineteen) and Moscow (at the age of twenty-two). He was accompanied in both cases by relatives[9].

As a corollary to Acton's respect for Döllinger went an equal respect for German scholarship: 'The greatest growth of intellectual life is in Germany,' runs an early note, 'and all that has been done in France or England for science is inspired by the Germans'[10].

In the narrow sense of the term, Acton's studies were over in 1858. In the wider sense he remained a student till the end of his days. The efforts that he made to keep abreast of all the latest developments in thought and natural science in the second half of the nineteenth century were a matter of constant wonder to his contemporaries. The man who wrote:

'... the full exposition of truth is the great object for which the existence of mankind is prolonged on earth'[11] was not himself likely to rest until he had mastered the truth.

All through his life also, Acton was more than eager to put his knowledge at the disposal of a wider circle. He did not conceive of his search for truth in isolation from practical activity. The 'desire to make a name for himself' that he had had as a schoolboy accompanied him into his twenties[12]. It coalesced with the desire to play some active role, to make some public impact, though not necessarily of a political nature.

On Acton's return to England his intention was to re-create the atmosphere of the Munich circle. He aspired to become the intellectual mentor of the English Catholics and to raise their standard of scholarship. He had plans for the establishment of a Roman Catholic University and for a Roman Catholic Historical Society to be named after the historian Lingard. As a first step towards the more general fulfilment of these aims, Acton assumed the editorship of a bi-monthly Catholic periodical *The Rambler*, later to be renamed as a quarterly *The Home and Foreign Review.*

He sought as contributors 'men who think for themselves and are not slaves to tradition and authority'[13]. This policy was to court trouble, all the more so as *The Rambler* had previously been suspect to the Catholic hierarchy for its deviations. Acton himself now did a great deal to confirm the hierarchy in its suspicion. He constantly reiterated in both journals that the Church, as the embodiment of absolute and eternal truth, had nothing to fear from the discovery of new scientific or historical truths in the temporal sphere. This thesis Acton carried to its farthest limits. He wrote, for example, that 'a discovery may be made in science which will shake the faith of thousands; yet religion cannot refute it or object to it'; or that 'a newly discovered truth may be a stumbling block to perplex or to alienate the minds of men. Is she (*i.e.* the Church) therefore to deny or to smother it? By no means. She must in every case do right'[14].

This attitude can be further illustrated from Acton's treatment of two systems of thought whose impact in the nineteenth century was to shake the faith of many – the evolutionary controversy and the historical criticism of the Bible. He had no hesitation in accepting both systems on their own merits, and in seeing nothing necessarily incompatible between either and his religion. He could write that a Catholic's religion 'is no more affected by the detection of a scandal in the Church than by the discovery of a fossil man, or of an African tribe whose heads do grow beneath their shoulders'[15]. In the field of Biblical criticism, one of Acton's many tributes to its researches is his estimate of the work of Ferdinand Christian Baur. 'The German intellect', he wrote, 'can boast of no greater achievement'[16]. Furthermore, Acton's identification of St Augustine as the spiritual father of Jansenism, or his attacks on the administration of the Papal states, were hardly of lesser importance. Within a very few years Acton had succeeded in drawing upon himself the hostility of his ecclesiastical superiors. As Dr Gooch has remarked, 'the position of a critical individualist in a Church claiming divine authority was intrinsically difficult'[17]. In 1862 *The Rambler* was suppressed.

It re-emerged the same year as *The Home and Foreign Review* with a precisely similar message. The new title did not of course allay suspicion and the first number of the quarterly provoked the old hostility. Cardinal Wiseman accused it of lacking 'all reserve or reverence in its treatment of persons or of things deemed sacred, its grazing over the very edges of the most perilous abysses of error, and its habitual preferences of uncatholic to catholic instincts, tendencies, and motives'. In making these remarks, the Cardinal, Acton's former headmaster at Oscott, emphasised that he was 'obeying a higher direction' than his own impulses[18]. This was a clear reference to Rome whence Wiseman had just returned.

There the same attitude prevailed with at least equal strength. In 1863, the year following Wiseman's speech, Döllinger incurred the same hostility as did Acton, and on a very similar issue. At a Catholic congress in Munich Döllinger had pleaded that the Church relax its enmity to historical criticism. In reply, in December, 1863, the Pope addressed a Brief or rescript to the Archbishop of Munich declaring the opinion of Catholic writers subject to Rome. The rescript was not published until March, 1864. But as soon as its contents became known, Acton at once realised that the death-knell had sounded for the *Home and Foreign Review* no less than for Döllinger's hopes. He wrote to Richard Simpson, his close collaborator on the *Review*, that it would lose 'the very breath of its nostrils.... There is nothing new in the sentiments of the rescripts; but the open aggressive declaration and the will to enforce obedience are in reality new. This is what places us in flagrant contradiction with the government of the Church'[19]. Acton had no alternative but to cease publication. He did not, however, abjure his convictions, as he made clear in his final article in the *Review*, entitled 'Conflicts with Rome.' 'I will sacrifice the existence of the *Review*', he wrote, 'to the defence of its principles, in order that I may combine the obedience which is due to legitimate ecclesiastical authority with an equally conscientious maintenance of the rightful and necessary liberty of thought'[20].

The necessity of this decision was reinforced later the same year. In December, 1854, the Pope had proclaimed the dogma of the Immaculate Conception. On the tenth anniversary of the new dogma he issued the Encyclical *Quanta Cura* together with an attached Syllabus of Errors. The errors included liberty of the press, liberty of worship, the separation of Church and State, socialism, communism and the belief that the Church should reconcile herself with progress, liberalism and modern civilisation. This sealed Acton's divorce from the hope of any influential position as a Catholic apologist. After six short years, during which his writings had been prodigious in volume and range, he was never to write again in a Catholic periodical. All his later efforts to influence his co-religionists were perforce made through non-Catholic publications or personal contact.

Acton's parliamentary career covered much the same years as his journalistic career. In 1859 Granville secured for his step-son the constituency of Carlow in Ireland which Acton represented until the General Election of 1865. He then stood for Bridgnorth near the family estate at Aldenham but in 1866 he was unseated on a recount. During his seven years in Parliament Acton limited himself to three questions, all concerned with Catholic affairs[21].

When the project of a seat for 'Johnny Acton' – as Granville called him – first came up, Granville wrote to his friend, Lord Canning, the Viceroy of India, that Acton had 'a yearning for public life'[22]. There must have been a misunderstanding here, for Acton left Granville in no doubt as to his distaste for politics. He wrote to him in terms that already suggest his later condemnation of the man of action. He wrote of the 'fastidiousness produced by long study which public life tends possibly to dissipate' and of his 'aversion' and 'incapacity for public life'[23]. As if to confirm this, Acton can be found meditating over the next few years on how to 'get out of Parliament in an honest way' in order to settle down amongst his books; or he complains that he cannot finish 'Nationality' until he is 'off' a railway committee[24].

The year 1865 marks a certain break in Acton's life. It followed on his exclusion from the Catholic press; it marked the virtual end of his Parliamentary career – there were to be no more burdensome railway committees – and it was also the year of his marriage. He married Countess Marie Arco-Valley, a relative on his mother's side[25]. It would seem that Lady Granville exerted pressure on her son in favour of Marie. A note in Acton's hand, dated 27th October 1859 – six years before the marriage took place – describes an interview between mother and son during an illness of the former; 'Then she said – *Et la petite Marie* – partly as a question. I made them leave me alone with her, and asked: "*Si j'avais l'espoir d'épouser Marie, est-ce-que vous l'aimeriez?*" These words seemed to give my poor mother more pleasure than anything which happened during my illness. This was when she had asked most eagerly – *Est-ce vraisemblable?* and I answered: *Je l'ai désiré beaucoup depuis des années.* She was extremely agitated with the pleasure this gave her, and seemed to have waited for it long'[26].

Although six children, of whom some died in infancy, were born of the marriage, it does not seem to have been a happy alliance. Acton was by character far too interested in ideas and the outside world to be much given to introspection. The very rare passages of this sort amongst his notes are thereby of enhanced significance. In a confused way, one such note speaks perhaps of an unhappy family and married life. Acton asks: 'May one resist the state? Or cashier a king? Or be husband of two wives? Or deceive a questioner? Or keep a slave? Or torture a prisoner? Or burn a witch? Or go to King Lear? Or back one's opinion?'[27]. It is apparent that his family life was not able to console him for the isolation of his later years.

The factor, which more than any other perhaps caused Acton's isolation, was the proclamation of Papal Infallibility in 1870. The new dogma had been in the air ever since the publication of the Encyclical *Quanta Cura* in 1864, and perhaps even before. Positions were soon taken up in preparation for the struggle. To Acton the menace of the threatened dogma lay foremost in the retrospective sanction it would confer on previous Papal decrees. As early as 1867 he attacked it on these lines. 'The Bulls which imposed a belief in the deposing power, the Bulls which prescribed the tortures and kindled the flames of the Inquisition . . . would become as venerable as the decrees of Nicaea, as incontrovertible as the writings of St Luke . . . the Church would take the place of a moon, reflecting passively the light which the Pope received directly from heaven'[28]. Döllinger's *The Pope and the Council* (written under the pseudonym of Janus) attacked the proposed dogma from another angle, that of the historian. Papal Infallibility, he maintained, had no historical sanction and defied the Church's tradition.

The long-heralded Council eventually assembled at the end of 1869, and remained in session until July, 1870. Acton, too, was in Rome for the bulk of this period. The extent of his fears can be gauged from a letter to Gladstone in which he described the Council as 'an organised conspiracy to establish a power which would be the most formidable enemy of liberty as well as of science throughout the world'[29]. Although with little expectation of success he continued to oppose the Pope's intention and became one of the contributors to a series of letters that Döllinger published in the *Augsburger Allgemeine Zeitung* under the pseudonym of Quirinus. The letters themselves were based on information supplied to Acton and his fellow-correspondents by those Bishops opposed to the new dogma. Their characteristic is a shrewd day-by-day analysis of the political technique employed to push the dogma through[30].

But it was all in vain. Acton's worst fears were realised when, in July, 1870, the dogma of Papal Infallibility was formally proclaimed: the Pope cannot err in defining in virtue of his apostolic authority and *ex cathedra* any doctrine of faith and morals. Acton had maintained his opposition to the end and on the promulgation of the decree sent to an unnamed German Bishop a 'Sendschreiben'. He attacked 'the flagrant contradiction' between 'the earlier speech' of the Opposition Bishops and 'their later silence'[31]. This reproach however, as Acton was only too well aware, touched him quite as deeply as those he attacked. Döllinger, despite the pain that it involved, refused to accept the dogma and thereby put himself into a position where excommunication was inevitable. It was for Döllinger 'a deliverance' since he had no intention of voluntarily cutting himself adrift from Rome[32]. Acton shared this sentiment to the full. He had as little intention as Döllinger of voluntarily leaving the Church. He wrote to *The Times*, in 1874, of the Church 'whose Communion is dearer to me than life'[33]. He did not on the other hand accept the new dogma. What happened in fact, was that he once again gave external obedience to the requirements of his faith without abandoning his hostile position. He explained in a note: 'The act (*i.e.* of submission) was one of pure obedience, and was not grounded on the removal of my motives of opposition to the decrees'[34].

The crisis through which Acton passed was never resolved. He emerged a broken man. He had come unmistakably to realise the gap between his vision of the Church and the reality of the Church. When he censured Macaulay for having '*plus de largeur que de subtilité ou de finesse*', or for showing too little awareness of '*les angoisses de la conscience*'[35], he could never himself be suspected of a like deficiency. If ever a man struggled with his conscience, that man was Acton. The precise form assumed by the '*angoisse*' was a constant tension between Acton's Catholicism and his critical mind. He passed the last thirty years of his life in a state of inner conflict. He has described it in unmistakable and moving terms, which show, once again, the nature of his ambitions: 'Men of original powers, finding that they cannot force their views on the world, adapt themselves to some one current, which they choose, not because it is their own. There is some compromise or concession. Again – a man of original mind, having begun in a religion not his own choice, finds that it is not entirely his own. He annihilates part, he leaves out part, he lives in some illusion, for a time – permanently, he compromises'[36]. This permanent compromise must have been all the more painful to Acton for he had a fierce hatred of any form of intellectual evasion. He had an extremely subtle mind and was well aware how white may shade into grey and grey shade into black. Yet at the same time he was also aware that in the last resort both black and white are distinguishable. The sheep can be separated from the goats. 'We may pursue several objects, we may weave many principles, but we cannot have two courts of final appeal'[37]. Yet this is precisely what Acton was trying to have.

Of these struggles the outside world knew little, if anything. Once the fight over Infallibility was concluded, Acton, apart from his unremitting study, settled down to the life of a gentleman of leisure. He travelled constantly between Aldenham, London, Cannes and Tegernsee, his wife's estate in Bavaria. Sub-branches, so to speak, of the main library at Aldenham were established on the Riviera and in Bavaria so that the business of study might not be interrupted. Acton became, too, a well-known figure at many London clubs – the Athenaeum, Grillions, the Literary Society, the Club. He belonged to the Dilettanti for a short while, and was also among the founders of the Breakfast Club[38]. A gift for spontaneous and playful humour, the ability to converse learnedly but lightly, an interest in worldly gossip, an appreciation of good food and wine all combined to make of him a thorough man of the world. One of his fellow club-men wrote of Acton: 'his learning was only a part of him. To make Acton you had to add, *inter alia*, his lightness of touch in conversation, his half-cynical playfulness, his power of making himself at home in all circles from the Court to the College, his curiously interesting range of European relations, and a certain glamour which many must have felt, but which none, I imagine, could define'[39]. Amongst Acton's English friends and acquaintances were Gladstone, Morley, Bryce, Lecky, Mackenzie Wallace (the famous *Times* correspondent in Russia), the historians Creighton and Stubbs, and many lesser personalities. In Germany he knew philosophers and historians of the stamp of Mommsen, Dilthey, Sybel, Ranke, Harnack, Bluntschli, Waitz and Giesebrecht. In France he is said to have known every prominent scholar with the exception of Guizot[40]. Perhaps Acton's closest friend was Lady Blennerhassett. She has been well described as 'his Egeria'[41]. Acton spoke of her in terms that apply with equal felicity to himself. He found her 'immensely intelligent . . . [and] at home in the Faubourg-St Germain'[42]. She was by birth the Countess of Leyden and had married Sir Roland Blennerhassett, one of Acton's former parliamentary colleagues. She shared many of Acton's intellectual interests and was the author of books and articles on Mme de Staël, Talleyrand, Cardinal Newman and Georges Sand. Her correspondence with Acton, now in English, now in French, is couched in more personal tones than was usual with him. When he died, she wrote no less than three lengthy obituaries.

In marked contrast with Acton's regular writings from 1858 to 1864, he published very little after 1870. Yet in spite of this – or perhaps *because* of this – he was the recipient of several distinguished academic awards. In 1872 he was awarded the honorary degree of Doctor of Philosophy at Munich; in 1888 Cambridge made him an honorary Doctor of Laws; in 1889 Oxford followed suit with the honorary degree of Doctor of Civil Laws; in 1890 he was elected to an honorary fellowship at All Souls'; and in 1892 Gladstone appointed him to the position of Lord-in-Waiting to Queen Victoria. The culminating point in Acton's surprising career was his nomination by Lord Rosebery to the Regius Professorship of Modern History at Cambridge.

These honours and distinctions must well have seemed to their recipient something of a mockery. Although Acton never said so, he utterly despised the circumstances in which he had cast his lot. A note speaks volumes for the tension subsisting between Acton and his immediate environment: 'It takes a gentleman to live on terms of hearty friendship and kindness and intimacy with men whose ideas and conduct he abhors, and of whom he well knows that they view with contempt the principle on which he shapes his own character and life'[43]. In these years two Actons came to exist: the first was the man of the world, and the second the frustrated scholar. In his heart of hearts, away from society, Acton was lonely, unhappy, and, above all, thwarted. The price that he paid for the honours he received was silence. It is tempting to see in the frequency of his references to sociological studies of suicide and his notation of the statistically favoured months the extent of this despair[44].

In the years from 1879 onwards this feeling of loneliness was reinforced by his growing alienation from Döllinger in a matter that to Acton was as much personal as historical – moral judgments in history. The final separation took place in 1882. Acton now felt and knew himself to be 'absolutely alone' in his 'essential ethical position'[45]. He withdrew more and more into his shell, quoting in justification perhaps a line from Alfred de Vigny's poem *La Mort du Loup: 'Seul le silence est grand; tout le reste est faiblesse'*[46].

At the same time, the earlier Acton, the young man who had dreamed of fame and of a public career was by no means dead. Not only did the later Acton follow every move made by his political hero, Gladstone, but he also took a keen interest in the political evolution of the Continent. He went even further and on several occasions essayed to take a direct part in politics in a way that was essentially and absolutely incompatible with his general views on politics. It is clear that the urge to action at times overcame his awareness of the immorality of political action. On one occasion Acton asked Gladstone when he intended to find a place for him in the Cabinet[47]. On another occasion he more or less suggested himself to Gladstone as the British representative at Munich. 'If you approved . . . of my appointment,' he wrote, 'I may, of course, fairly say that there are no complications between this country and Bavaria that would give me any opportunity for mismanagement; and I not only know Germany pretty well, but I enjoy a measure of favour with the Royal Family. You will laugh, but it is a fact, due to family and social connexions'[48]. Utopian-emotional factors distorted his intellectual insight.

The effect of isolation was all the more fatal in that it

coincided with the years when Acton was hoping to settle down to his life's work, 'The History of Liberty'. This has been unkindly dubbed the greatest book that never was written. Döllinger once said that if Acton did not write a *magnum opus* before he was forty (1874) he would never do so. The prophecy was fulfilled. It does not even seem that Acton seriously tried to write his 'History'. Not even the plan of a plan exists[49]; and as early as 1882 Acton and Mary Gladstone were referring in their correspondence to the projected work as 'the Madonna of the Future'[50]. What was the reason for this?

The fact of the matter is that there was a certain streak of pliability in Acton's nature. He lacked the courage of his convictions. He had not the strength to tread a lonely and possibly painful path – but preferred silence. The same curiously repeated pattern can be detected on three occasions in Acton's life: his acquiescence in a course of action with which he is not in agreement. He had not agreed with the suspension of the *Home and Foreign Review* – but he none the less complied with the wishes of the hierarchy. He had not wanted a seat in the House of Commons – but he none the less fell in with Granville's plans. He had not agreed with the dogma of Infallibility – but he none the less accepted it. His marriage may also come into this category. Doubtless, were more biographical details available, the same pattern could be traced yet further. In all these cases, of course, it is easy to understand the motives that moved Acton to act as he did. Yet it is also easy to see that repeated compromises cannot be indulged in without incurring the possible loss of intellectual integrity. It was not for nothing that Acton asked: 'May one . . . back one's opinion?' or that he warned himself: 'Never lose the passionate love of what is ideal, noble, sublime'[51].

The compromise in Acton's life was naturally reflected in his work. He constantly lamented his lack of contemporaries[52], meaning by this the lack of sympathy he found for his views. But Acton did not for this reason try and form his own school, as it were. He had once run foul of authority. He would not do so again. He kept quiet in the full awareness that he was shirking the struggle. If there is a redeeming aspect of Acton's pliability, it is the honesty with which he faced the position. He never sought to impose upon himself. He wrote, for example, to Bishop Creighton: 'If I tried to work out in detail and to justify my theory of history, I should only lose all my friends, so that I am linked to the penumbra'[53]. The way in which this worked out in practice can be seen just as clearly in the relatively trivial matter of a discussion between Acton and Jowett about Macaulay as in the vastly more important dispute with Döllinger on morality and history. In describing his reaction to both incidents, Acton was as frank as in his letter to Creighton.

It was in these terms that Acton described his encounter with Jowett. He wrote to Mary Gladstone: 'You remember that conversation with Jowett about Macaulay. I thought Macaulay thoroughly dishonest and insincere and had a variety of reasons, good or bad, for my opinion. At the first, I discovered that Jowett was surprised, almost hurt. *So I shut up as soon as I could.* They must have thought that I had not much to say, that I could not produce a single passage from his books in my support, that I came to conclusions too quickly, rather from a latent prejudice than on evidence.

What, in such a case, should a good man do? *Surely he prefers discomfiture to a fight that is likely to be both tiresome and painful. He will put on no more steam than the thing is worth*, and will not mind people being in the wrong if he is not responsible for them. When no higher question is involved, he will not strive for victory'[54].

The relationship of morality to history meant vastly more to Acton than Macaulay's status as a historian. Even so, he was no more prepared to fight for his views here than in the case of Macaulay. The actual content of the views is to be discussed later. Here it is only necessary to note that they were such as to involve a complete breach with Döllinger. But when this fact became apparent to Acton he once again gave up the attempt to persuade – and relapsed into silence. The conclusion that he drew from the clash with Döllinger was this: 'The probability of doing good by writings so isolated and repulsive . . . is so small that I have no right to sacrifice to it my own tranquillity and my duty of educating my children. My time can be better employed than in waging a hopeless war. And the more my life has been thrown away, the more necessary to turn now and employ better what remains. I am absolutely alone in my essential ethical position and therefore useless'[55].

In a word, the reason why Acton did not write his 'History of Liberty' lay in his lack of courage to affront a hostile world unaided. In his own words, he would only 'lose all his friends'; he preferred 'discomfiture to a tiresome and painful struggle'; he refused 'to sacrifice his tranquillity'. It is in these circumstances no matter for surprise that so many of Acton's dicta have the air of being a wild release from the tension of frustration.

Acton turned on himself the same disenchanted gaze that he turned on others. To Mary Gladstone he as much as confessed that his silence arose from lack of support. He spoke of his 'tiresome book' and asked her to remember that 'I can only say things which people do not agree with, that I have neither disciple nor sympathiser, that this is no encouragement to production or confidence ... and that I have no other gift but that which you pleasantly describe, of sticking eternal bits of paper into innumerable books, and putting larger papers into black boxes. There is no help for it. But your reproaches are much more distressing to read than you suppose ...'[56]. Lady Blennerhassett, in one of her three obituaries of Acton, strongly suggests this diagnosis from the outside. 'If', she wrote in the *Edinburgh Review*, 'he had met with understanding and sympathy, he would perhaps have overcome his natural dislike for limited themes and for composition as circumscribed within the limits of a book'[57].

As it was, Acton did not overcome his dislike for limited themes, even though some of them – *e.g.* his article 'German Schools of History' – contains, as he said in another connection, 'the squashed material of a proper volume'[58]. He was again too honest with himself to yield to self-pity; for he knew that the thwarting of his hopes was, in the last resort, self-imposed. If there is an exception to this, it can perhaps be seen in a list of historians he drew up under the title – 'Persecuted Professors of History.' Beside the list, Acton has written: 'How little encouragement!'[59]

Acton did not, of course, cease publishing altogether during these lonely years. Yet when he did do so, he was confronted with a peculiar predicament. Acton was the last man in the world to contradict what he believed to be the truth. On the other hand, he was afraid to express his beliefs precisely in the form in which he held them. There is many a nuance and many a subtlety between these two extremes. In this indeterminable field Acton was a perpetual wanderer. Again he knew what he was doing. Three occasions are on record when he confessed to having diluted his views for publication. They are all contained in letters to Creighton, the first editor of the *English Historical Review*, where all the reviews in question appeared. The first concerns Dr Franz von Wegele's *Geschichte der deutschen Historiographie*, which was the peg whereon Acton hung *German Schools of History*. When the book was first submitted to Acton for review he wrote to Creighton: 'I can say all I know and can get my knife into every joint without being felt.' After the review had appeared (in 1886) and had evoked some criticism, Acton, in another letter to Creighton, informed him how he had carried out this strange operation: '*when I disagreed I seldom said so*, but rather tried to make out a possible case in favour of views I don't share. Nobody can be more remote than I am from the Berlin and Tübingen schools; but I tried *to mark my disagreement by the lightest touch*. From the Heidelberg school I think there is nothing to learn and I said so'. The second occasion concerned Viscount Bryce's *The American Commonwealth*. Here Acton wrote that he had marked his disagreement with Bryce '*with the least possible assertion of difference* ... in a way some readers, I suppose, will not understand. But there is some material for meditation for the thinking reader'. The third occasion concerns Creighton's own *History of the Papacy*. The original draft of Acton's review of this work was even more violently hostile than the version which eventually appeared. Even so, in referring to this first draft, he wrote to Creighton: '... I thought I had contrived *the gentlest formula of disagreement* in coupling you with Cardinal Newman'[60]. What happened in these cases may reasonably be conjectured to have happened in others.

To cope with the necessity of getting his knife into every joint without being felt, Acton developed a quite peculiar style. There is perhaps no greater contrast between the young and the mature Acton than in this matter of style. What was in youth flowing and diffuse became in maturity crabbed, tortuous, contorted, elliptic and allusive. 'Clearness, a French disease' runs one of the notes[61]. It is certainly not a malady from which Acton can be said to have suffered. Few students of his writings have failed to comment on this. Morley found him 'fatally addicted to the oblique and the allusive'[62]. And even Creighton who was, after all, a historian and therefore accustomed to making out the meaning of the most misleading documents found Acton 'enigmatical' and 'terribly obscure'[63]. Freeman, another historian, once told Acton that one could not tell whether his review of the Reverend Bright's *History of England* was favourable or not[64].

It is, in these circumstances, to the notes that recourse must be had if the authentic Acton is to be comprehended. *There* he was under no obligation to trade in nuances or enigmatic subtleties. *There* he could be as candid as he wanted. *There* no ray of a possibly unfavourable daylight could penetrate. For this reason, whereas drafts, notes, etc, may normally be considered as a prelude and preparation for what is to be published, and hence subject to revision before receiving their final form, in Acton's case the contrary is valid. *His* notes represent what he would like to have said, and *his* published works constitute what is blurred and incomplete. But it must again be emphasised, there is no question of contradiction, rather of nuance[65].

If the worst that can be said of Acton is that he lacked the courage of his convictions, the best must speak of his intellectual capacity. No account of his life could ever be complete that did not do some justice, however inadequate, to his vast learning and scholarship. He was at home in a dozen different fields of knowledge, and could write and converse in English, French, German and Italian. He had, in addition, a knowledge of the two classical languages.

Stories of Acton's erudition are legion. Maitland, a professorial colleague at Cambridge, thought him capable of writing unaided the twelve volumes of the Cambridge Modern History[66]. Gladstone would refer to Acton for the final word whenever any point of dispute arose in conversation. Bryce noted of a dinner where Creighton and Robertson Smith were fellow-guests with Acton that he knew as much of Pope Leo X as the former, and as much of the controversies in the dating of the books of the Old Testament as the latter. Both Creighton and Smith were specialists in their respective subjects[67]. Morley had an even more surprising experience. 'Once, after a great political gathering in a country town, owing to some accident of missing carriages, he (*i.e.* Acton) and I had to walk home three or four miles along a country road. I mentioned that I had engaged to make a discourse at Edinburgh on Aphorisms. This fired him, and I was speedily and joyfully on the scent of a whole band of German, French, Italian and Spanish names ample enough to carry me through half a score discourses. I never had a shorter walk'[68].

The well whence Acton drew his knowledge was a magnificent library of some sixty thousand volumes. Yet it looked like a bookshop and many of the volumes were bound for one and sixpence apiece[69]. The fact is that Acton distrusted mere appearance and, indeed, warned the hypothetical young man, for whom his list of the Hundred Best Books was intended, 'to steel' himself against literary beauty and charm[70]. Acton's interests were overwhelmingly intellectual. He had not only a basic classical knowledge; he combined this with a thorough knowledge of the whole body of thought of his own time and of that of the preceding three or four centuries. Acton's notes contain, cheek by jowl, quotations from Rabelais and Adam Smith, Vico and Marx,

Spinoza and Machiavelli, Ranke and Diderot, Dilthey and Guizot, Gladstone and Alfred de Vigny, Schleiermacher and St Thomas Aquinas, Burke and Pascal, Leibniz and Sainte Beuve, Kant and Dr Johnson, Sheridan and Edmond Schérer, Taine and Hegel, Montaigne and Newman, Stahl and Descartes, Bishop Butler and Voltaire, Gibbon and George Eliot, D. F. Strauss and Kirkegaard, Bossuet and Burckhardt, Tocqueville and Lassalle, Mme de Staël and Windelband, Lamennais and Mme de Sévigné, Matthew Arnold and Bacon, Bakunin and Cournot, Gustave Le Bon and Krafft-Ebbing, Spencer and Hobbes, to say nothing of innumerable theologians and countless lesser-known historians, philosophers, economists, jurists, essayists and literary critics.

II: THE HISTORICAL BACKGROUND

In the same way as Acton's personal and biographical background makes it difficult to include him in any 'national' category, so do the ramifications of his intellectual background make it difficult to place him in any tradition or school of historiography. On both counts he was something of a curiosity. The man who numbered amongst his immediate ancestors and relatives a cardinal, a member of the Cabinet, a Bourbon Prime Minister, and a Napoleonic Duke, had at the same time a personal culture of such complexity that at first sight it seems almost to be coterminous with the intellectual history of European man.

Moreover, the effect of this background in abstracting Acton from the pressure of his immediate environment was reinforced and confirmed by the need he experienced to define and elaborate his own position *vis-à-vis* history. He was not, perhaps, aware of all the philosophical problems involved in the writing of history. On the other hand, he was also not a naïve historian, contenting himself with the accepted methods and aims of his time. Acton knew little, if any, of the harmony between man and environment that had characterised, for example, the work of Gibbon or Macaulay. He himself was not in a position where he could epitomise in his work, as they had done, the outlook and values of the environment in its doctrine of man, religion, politics, no less than of history itself. He knew none of the popularity and corresponding rewards that had come their way.

Even less was Acton a 'Dryasdust'. Indeed, he complained that it was the historian's 'professional curse' to have to read so many 'worthless books' that 'a man afraid of being bored is as unfit for a historian as a fisherman'[71]. It is, furthermore, a noteworthy and obvious feature of almost all his book reviews and review articles that they are as much concerned with the author's attitude or philosophy as with his narrative, text, authorities, style, etc. Generalising reflections are equally obviously a feature of his own historical writings.

No, neither a 'Dryasdust' nor a historian content to work within a traditional framework, Acton was that rare bird – a reflective historian. Living and writing in the second half of the nineteenth century, he was both heir to and contemporary with the century *par excellence* of historical writing. In Great Britain, there were Macaulay and Carlyle; in Germany, Niebuhr, Ranke, Mommsen, Treitschke; in France, Michelet, Taine and Renan. Through the reasearch and narrative powers of historians such as these, and their many followers and contemporaries, vast new tracts of human experience were disclosed. The history of religion, culture, ideas, institutions, as well as of politics, diplomacy and states, became in many cases accessible for the first time. No other age, probably, had witnessed a comparable extension of knowledge in so many fields in so short a time.

It was against this achievement that Acton had to define his own position. Above all, he had to work out his answer to the romanticism, or historicism, that characterised the nature of the nineteenth century achievement. However great Acton's appreciation of the contribution made by romanticism to 'the full exposition of truth', which he saw as 'the great object for which the existence of man is prolonged on earth'[72], he could not yield it unreserved tribute.

A quotation from his Inaugural Lecture as Regius Professor of Modern History, delivered at Cambridge in 1895, shows something of the impact, not to say fascination, exercised on Acton by the romantic movement in history. He is speaking of the share taken by scholars of other disciplines in creating the romantic atmosphere encompassing and permeating historiography: 'The jurists brought us that law of continuous growth which has transformed history from a chronicle of casual occurrences into the likeness of something organic. Towards 1820 divines began to recast their doctrines on the lines of development.... Even the economists, who were practical men, dissolved their science into liquid history, affirming that it is not an auxiliary, but the actual subject-matter of their enquiry. Philosophers claim that, as early as 1804, they began to bow the metaphysical neck beneath the historical yoke. They taught that philosophy is only the amended sum of all philosophies, that systems pass with the age whose impress they bear, that the problem is to focus the rays of wandering but extant truth, and that history is the source of philosophy, if not quite a substitute for it. Comte begins a volume with the words that the preponderance of history over philosophy was the characteristic of the time he lived in. Since Cuvier first recognised the conjunction between the course of inductive discovery and the course of civilisation, science had its share in saturating the age with historic ways of thought, and in subjecting all things to that influence for which the depressing names historicism and historical-mindedness have been devised"[73].

This description sufficiently indicates the strength of the romantic impact confronting Acton. But why were historicism and historical-mindedness 'depressing names'? What was the source of the disharmony between Acton's age, 'saturated with historic ways of thought', and his own dislike of historical-mindedness? This is the core of the conflict between Acton and his time – romanticism was too powerful and too valuable to be neglected, and yet too dangerous to be accepted. Acton had to remove its sting before he could enjoy its benefits.

To understand this more fully, it is necessary to give some sketchy account of the romantic outlook. What exactly was Acton fighting against? Briefly then, in so far as history was concerned, it visualised the past less as a static and finished product, capable of becoming the source of historical laws and generalisations, and more as a phase in human history, carrying within itself the foreshadowing of the future, which in its turn would foreshadow yet another future. Romantic writers, therefore, tended to delve into the origins of things, for it was only from this standpoint that the course of subsequent developments could fully be comprehended. Thus, as a further consequence, a certain *mystique* came to envelop the past as such, for this was also in a certain sense the present. The quest for origins and roots was to such an extent one aspect of romantic historiography that the movement has sometimes received the name of the genetic movement in history.

Equally important to historians was the romantic emphasis on the ever-developing nature of historical reality. Henceforth, they were not dealing with something outside the flow of time but with something that essentially constituted the very flow of time, of which they themselves were but another constituent. The course of life itself became identified with the subject-matter of history. It was in this way that historians turned aside from the timeless categories and rationalist *a priori* explanations of the eighteenth century Enlightenment to seek out what was unique, individual and characteristic, what was redolent of '*la couleur locale*' of any particular epoch at any particular phase of human development. Amongst the romantic historians there developed a new sense of the freshness and richness of the past, and above all of the Middle Ages, the object of the Enlightenment's especial scorn as an era of backward superstition.

This altered aim and approach inevitably called into play faculties different from those hitherto employed. In particular, there was a heightened appreciation of feeling and sympathy as a means of understanding. 'Nowhere before our time do I find the immediate feeling for the life of the past . . .' wrote Renan. 'Our century was the first to have that kind of finesse which groups, with the apparently colourless uniformity of ancient accounts, traits of manners and character which no longer have similarities in the present state of society'[74]. This 'finesse', this 'immediate feeling for the life of the past', was the chosen instrument of the romantic historian for grasping and entering into the spirit of the past – itself a suggestive key-phrase of the movement.

Finally, and by far the most important, was the implicit presupposition of historicism. This was the absence of any presupposition on the part of the historian, for only thus could he allow full and adequate scope to the development of the faculty of 'finesse', of understanding. He could clearly not surrender himself to his material with the necessary abandon if he had not previously emancipated himself from his own views and predilections. These would otherwise have the inevitable effect of acting as a barrier between himself and his material. They would disturb and distort the exercise of understanding. He had to have the capacity of reacting to the past with something of the impartiality of a barometer, as it were, recording the state of the atmosphere. Advancing on these lines, romanticism soon became, at least as far as Acton was concerned, synonymous with relativism. For if the romantic expressly had no scale of values of his own, then he had perforce to adopt those of history itself, *i.e.* to see history in its own light. But as history showed every conceivable variety of value and behaviour and since there was by definition no other world than that of history, then the historian could only depict a discordant and conflicting chaos of values. Whatever he encountered became history and thereby removed from the possibility of judgment and thereby relativised. The romantic movement in history culminated in Ranke's epigram – '*jede Epoche ist unmittelbar zu Gott*' – all the centuries are equal in the sight of God.

Such were some of the main features of the historicist background against which Acton had to define his own position. Of course no nineteenth century historian subscribed to them all. Many indeed, and especially those religiously inclined, had no thought of not writing from their individual points of view. Nevertheless, the movement enjoyed sufficient homogeneity and created a wide enough impact for its presence to be unmistakable.

Acton's counter-attack is dealt with in detail below. But it is important to see its motivation, and, therefore, to see the particular form that it took. It bore, above all, on the key-principle of romanticism that history in the sense of what happens is legitimised when it becomes history in the sense of historiography.

It is doubtless part of the very stuff of the historian's outlook that he should take his subject-matter for granted. Doubtless all historians are 'Whigs' in that they have a tendency 'to praise revolutions provided they have been successful, to emphasise certain principles of progress in the past and to produce a story which is the ratification if not the glorification of the present'[75]. Doubtless, merely through the brute fact of recording an event, of tracing and explaining its causes, the historian becomes inclined to see the event as justified or inevitable. He is impelled, willy-nilly, to set the stamp of his approval on the past. This must be all the more the case if the historian is a romantic, intent on self-identification with history.

Yet to Acton this attitude was intolerable; it imposed the neglect of certain values that for him stood beyond history. It reduced man to a mere historical being and removed his activity to a level devoid of value. He called in non-history to redress the balance of history. He could not, nor did he wish to, reject entirely the teachings of romanticism. But at the same time, because it implicitly or explicitly left out of account that aspect of human experience not limited to the historical – because, ultimately, it saw history from the standpoint of history itself and not from some external point – he was forced to develop an attitude that brought him into conflict with the bulk of his contemporaries. How he contrived to do this, whilst simultaneously retaining the achievements of the historicist outlook, forms the setting in which his own view of history can best be appreciated.

CHAPTER I

The Early Acton

THE phrase – 'the early Acton' – has to be taken with a certain amount of qualification. No clear dividing-line can be drawn between what he believed in his youth and what he believed in his maturity. These two major phases, as well no doubt, as many that are minor, dovetail well-nigh imperceptibly into one another. Furthermore, the difficulty of distinguishing one phase from another is intensified by the erratic tempo of Acton's publishing. From 1864-1867 for example, virtually the only known expression of his views was a public lecture delivered at Bridgnorth, near Aldenham.

Even so, making every allowance for these limiting circumstances, there is an unmistakable difference between the views of the early and of the mature Acton. The dividing line seems to fall around 1870, or perhaps a little before. This would be when he was in his early thirties, and would approximately coincide with the critical period of the Dogma of Infallibility, together with all the doubts and revaluations that it provoked. The difference between the two Actons can be traced further in the relative importance of two basic tendencies in his thought. Neither entirely disappeared, but whereas in the earlier period one was so strong as almost to obscure the other, in the later period the position was reversed. The fact of the co-existence throughout his life of two identical themes is in itself sufficient indication of the lack of any absolute break in Acton's development.

What were these two themes or tendencies? No overall formulation would be able to do them full justice. But a convenient and necessarily simplified *point de départ* can be found in Acton's attitude towards the world. Was the world to be confronted with ideal claims or was it to be fundamentally accepted? Whereas most young men begin with revolution and end with counter-revolution, Acton trod the contrary path. It was as a counter-revolutionary that he began and as a revolutionary that he ended. But in each phase he was *sui generis*. His counter-revolution was tinged with revolution, and *vice versa*.

Acton formed his first views under the influence of Edmund Burke, and especially of the later Burke. He described Burke's speeches of 1790-1795 as 'the law and the prophets'[1]; and in one of his earliest letters to Gladstone he wrote that the political purpose of the *Home and Foreign Review* was 'to maintain that old Whig system of which Burke is the great exponent'[2]. This unqualified admiration for Burke did not survive into Acton's later thought. The time was to come when Acton, whilst retaining many of Burke's insights, would condemn him as strongly as he now admired him. Indeed he 'would have hanged Mr Burke on the same gallows as Robespierre'[3]. But while the impact lasted, it was extremely potent, to such an extent that much of Burke's phraseology can be found closely mirrored in Acton's own writing.

Acton's view of Burke was not original. He saw him *par excellence* as the voice of tradition, in the widest sense of the term, and as the voice of the *status quo*. Burke stood remote from those who would impose on society a theoretically conceived pattern. He was the epitome of the man who shunned metaphysical and abstract criteria of rights and doctrines. He was guided by the past, in the conviction that the slow creation of time could not but be immeasurably superior to the mere impact of human wisdom. Burke came to terms with the world, not because he saw it as necessarily the best of all possible worlds, but because he saw it as the best world possible in the given circumstances. Finally, it was because Burke set so much store by the gradual accommodation of realities to ideals, and so determinedly opposed the violent imposition of a model order in the service of a single idea that Acton saw in him 'a purely Catholic view of political principles and of history'[4]. The action of the Church on society took precisely the same form. In reference to politics therefore Acton sometimes used the terms English (*i.e.* Burkeian) and Catholic as synonymous[5].

Acton could write: 'I cannot conceive a state in which reform should not be a normal condition of progress, that is, of existence'[6]. On the other hand, he could also indicate with precision within what limits reform might be accomplished: 'polity grows like language and is part of a people's nature, not dependent on its will. One or the other can be developed, modified, corrected; but they cannot be subverted or changed by the people itself without an act of suicide . . . if States would live, they must preserve their organic connection with their origin and history, which are their root and their stem; . . . they are not voluntary creations of human wisdom; . . . men labour in vain who would construct them without acknowledging God as the artificer'[7].

If the theme of organic reform as against revolution in Acton's early writings clearly shows this origin, there is another theme, which, though it may also derive ultimately from Burke, is given by Acton a far greater emphasis: it is the theme of power. Burke, who died in 1797, had seen neither the nationalist reaction to Napoleon nor the revolutions of 1848. Acton, writing in the late 1850's and early 1860's, had seen both. From this lengthened historical perspective he was able to discern the development of nationalism – or nationality, as Acton termed it – in a way necessarily hidden from Burke. The French Revolution, in Acton's view, had formed the watershed in this development, dividing the old Europe from the new. Its 'substance' had been 'not the limitation of the sovereign power but the abrogation of intermediate powers'[8]. This force had subsequently been overcome and overtaken by that of nationality. The theory of nationality which in 1789 had played no part in the revolution had now become 'its most advanced form'[9]. From the conjunction of these two forces Acton anticipated 'the modern danger . . . state-absolutism, not royal-absolutism'[10]. The end-result of this process would be a state where no intermediate powers hindered the expression of the will of the people. It was in the liberal, the equalitarian, the nationalist, the democrat, or the socialist with his 'school of universal administration'[11], that Acton saw the enemy.

It was from the same point of view that he judged the issues involved in the American Civil War (1861-1865). His discussion of what was a contemporary event – he termed it the American Revolution – illustrates further the purport of his views. His analysis has been termed by an American scholar 'over-simplified, if not worse'[12]. This is not necessarily a defect in the present context, for the over-simplification allows Acton's views to emerge crystal-clear. Acton unequivocally condemned the Northern abolitionists as a sort of American pendant to the French Jacobins. They exhibited an 'abstract, ideal absolutism which is equally hostile with the Catholic and with the English spirit. Their democratic system poisons everything it touches. All constitutional questions are referred to the one fundamental principle of popular sovereignty, without consideration of policy or expediency . . . In claiming absolute freedom, they have created absolute powers . . . The same intolerance of restraints and obligations, the same aversion to recognise the existence of popular duty, and of the divine right which is its correlative, disturb their notion of government and of freedom'[13]. The South, on the other hand, was conservative and the repository of 'the remnants of English traditions and institutions'[14]. Moreover, through the institution of slavery it resisted the baneful democratic doctrine of the Rights of Man.

Into his activity as a book reviewer Acton carried the same attitude. He concerned himself quite as much with the political or philosophical views of the author as with questions of text, authorities, etc. He maintained as a general proposition that the new historical materials everywhere becoming available in Europe were being 'forged into weapons by eager disputants'[15]. From his own standpoint he was forthright in correcting the balance, expressing himself in vigorous contrast to the enigmatic style of his later reviews.

Nationalist historians were to Acton the foremost of the 'eager disputants'. They were dealing with what to him was a quite unhistorical unit – the nation – on a spurious historical basis. The nation was barely seventy or eighty years old, dating from the partition of Poland or the French Revolution. Yet this truly revolutionary innovation was already being treated as a measure in its own right. Acton's sympathy was accordingly restricted to writers who treated with 'rightful scorn the sonorous principles of nationality and geographical limits'[16]. Thus he congratulated Bernhardt, the author of *Preussens Moderne Entwicklung*, for not concealing how the Great Elector 'sought an alliance with France at the very moment when Lewis XIV was endeavouring by "reunions" to detach flourishing parts from the body of the Empire'[17]. This may usefully be contrasted with Acton's treatment of Droysen's *Geschichte der preussischen Politik:* 'Their papers,' he wrote (referring to the papers of the Hohenzollern Dynasty) 'have not been entrusted to the historian that he may, if he see cause, diminish the lustre that surrounds their heroes, or exalt their rivals: but that he may make the best of a complicated case, and extract political influence out of chequered tradition. The History of Prussian Policy is in fact a conspiracy such as every nation has to blush for in its literature'[18]. Other examples of a similar tendency came from Russia and England. Of a work by Buturlin and Danilewsky on the Russian military archives for 1812 – the year of Russia's victory over Napoleon – Acton wrote that the two authors 'ministered to the national pride and imperial infallibility'[19]. The English example came from the *Letters of the First Earl of Malmesbury*. Acton commented: 'Perhaps it is only a peculiar view of international relations that leads Lord Malmesbury to describe England as "saving the Danish fleet by force from the grip of Napoleon in 1807" (vol. ii, p. 205). Danes are apt to view the matter differently'[20].

To the spirit of nationality embodied in such writings and to what Acton termed 'state absolutism' as its final result, the antidote was of course the existence of the maximum number of 'intermediate powers': and of these the foremost was the Church. Her prelates, in Acton's views, were not animated by 'the disinterested love of liberty'. At one time, he added, 'they sought to substitute a depotism of priests for the tyranny of kings'. Even so, in spite of herself, the Church was 'the parent-source of modern freedom'. She limited authority in the state 'by the immunity of a corporation strong enough for resistance, permanent in its organisation, constant in its maxims and superior to national boundaries'[21]. It was when Burke spoke in a similar strain of institutions and usages, sanctified by time and resisting man-made constitutions, that Acton saw in him 'the wisest . . . of all the advocates of the Catholic cause'[22].

Acton's argument for the political value of the Church, considered entirely apart from the divine content of course, committed him, again on political grounds, to a defence of Catholic persecution. He did not hesitate to take this step. On the several occasions when he dealt with the extermination of such heretics as the Albigenses and Waldenses, he was always able to justify their suppression. In an age when unity of Church and State existed, the Church, in taking up arms against heresy was not doing so from religious motives. She was repressing the forces of anarchy, such as would tear asunder the fabric of Christian society. The war against the Albigenses, for example, was 'not a purely religious war'. Their tenets 'were dangerous not as religious only but as social'[23]. In a lengthy review-article in *The Rambler* of a work by Döllinger on the temporal power of the Papacy, Acton expanded this argument. 'Every heresy,' he wrote, 'that arose in the Middle Ages involved revolutionary consequences, and would inevitably have overthrown State and Society as well as Church, wherever it prevailed. The Albigenses, who provoked the cruel legislation against heretics, and who were exterminated by fire and sword, were the Socialists of those days. They assailed the fundamental institutions of society, marriage, family and property and their triumph would have plunged Europe into the barbarism and licence of pagan times. The principle of the Waldenses and the Lollards were likewise incompatible with European civilisation'[24].

With this defence of Catholic persecution firmly established, Acton vigorously took up the cudgels against Protestant persecution. He found the *tu quoque* argument as between Catholics and Protestants 'inadmissible'. When the Catholics persecuted, their action was rooted in the requirements of society. This could not, argued Acton, be said of the Protestants. When they persecuted, not only did they deny the theoretical rights of the individual conscience; they also 'placed the necessity of intolerance on the simple ground of religious error'. It was 'a purely subjective test, and a purely revolutionary system'. It contradicted the system of Catholic intolerance, for this was 'handed down from an age when unity subsisted, and when its preservation, being essential for that of society, became a necessity of State as well as a result of circumstances'[25].

The conception of history that corresponded to the Burkeian view of the world shared the same characteristic of conformity. To question the autonomous status of history by raising the matter of moral standards, for example, was excluded. Thus one passage in an early notebook reads: 'Superfluity of moral standards in history. We are not wiser when we know that one is good or bad, but what are the causes and effects of his life. It is the business of Him to judge who can carry his judgement into effect'[26]. Elsewhere Acton censured Goldwin Smith for discussing 'the morality of men and actions far oftener than history . . . either requires or tolerates . . . Method not genius, or eloquence, or erudition, makes the historian'[27]. And what was method? Another early note seems to indicate that it was 'the organic division and arrangement of history' such as could be made 'the criterion of an universal history'[28]. The evidence does not suggest that Acton's theory of history had gone much beyond these very general reflections.

What has been said above represents without question the dominant strain in the pre-1870 Acton. But it was not the only strain and not so dominant as to obscure another Acton who held views entirely at variance with the *general* tenor of his outlook. The importance of the other Acton at this time lies not so much in his views in themselves but rather in the manner in which they embryonically pre-figure the mature Acton of the 1880's and 1890's.

The autonomy of politics formed the dividing line. In sympathy with Burke, Acton was obliged to separate the political world from abstract questions of right and wrong, morality and immorality, etc. The explicit antithesis in his study of the American Civil War was 'abstract, ideal absolutism' as against 'consideration of policy or expediency'. He could have done nothing else. Yet in spite of this rejection Acton was himself something of an abstract idealist – not in the sense of a Jacobin or an abolitionist, for example, but on an avowedly non-political basis. If one Acton took the fundamental political dispute of his time – and perhaps of all time – to be between Burke and the revolution, then there was also another Acton who took an independent stand whence the differences separating the two antagonists became less important and their similarities more important. This independent position can be roughly described as moral. At first infrequently, but more and more often as time went on, Acton applied to politics and to political personalities moral criteria in such a way as to blur the differences between, say, the revolutionaries and monarchists. He wrote, for example: 'There is a vast difference between the amount of misery inflicted by the

French Revolution and by the absolutism of the old monarchy; but there is an intense similarity of features and character between the crimes of the Revolutionists and the crimes of the Legitimists. The ancient monarchy does not stand higher in *political ethics* than the Republic'[29].

In the same spirit many of Acton's political dicta of this time are applicable indifferently to either side. When he called attention to 'vice in persons of exalted station'[30] he did not differentiate between one side and its opponent. Again, if it is true, as Acton wrote, that 'public statements of policy may be intended to influence opinion; secret directives are meant to control action'[31] then the stricture is such as to fall without distinction of party.

These are relatively trivial examples in comparison with the scornful terms of a review of Grant Duff's *Glance Over Europe*. The review was tantamount to a rejection of Acton's own past. He compared those politicians who imagined 'politics to be a merely empirical art' with the alchemists and astrologers in the history of chemistry and astronomy. Such politicians denied, as did their 'scientific' parallel in a different sphere, that politics 'corresponds to other sciences, such as political economy and jurisprudence, and is made up of scientific truths and ethical obligations'. Acton then illustrated his argument with an example from *Glance Over Europe:* 'Russia, says Mr Grant Duff, can no more afford to give up Warsaw than Great Britain can give up Dublin and therefore he thinks that we ought to sympathise neither with the Poles nor with the Fenians. The idea apparently is that progress depends on great concentrated powers. If there is any wrong, any oppression, any suffering, it is better to bear it than to impede with microscopic interests the majestic march of civilisation. Mr Grant Duff is averse to a judicial or legal way of looking at public events, and he is not willing to entertain the question of right apart from the question of progress... The precepts of a domestic morality will not do to judge the world by...'[32].

To the view that politics was not an affair of alchemy and astrology but was made up of 'scientific truths and ethical obligations' there was again an equivalent conception of history. This, too, would become an affair of truths and ethics. The seeds of this view may be seen in Acton's criticism of the 'dignified isolation' that Ranke imposed on history. It involved, Acton held, 'a certain poverty in the reflections, a certain inadequacy of generalisation'[33]. The same point is made with greater emphasis and clarity in his review of a Mr Knight's *Popular History of England*. The review is so important as to merit a generous extract. 'Mr Knight,' wrote Acton, 'exhibits a sort of liberality which will make his work popular but which is one of the gravest faults a historian can be guilty of.... He mistakes a generous suavity of temper for that many-sided sympathy which enables the historian to distribute equal justice, and to recognise, in every party and every opinion, that element of reason which gives it power over honest minds. Like a man conscious of weakness, he avoids temptation – he does not overcome it. His fairness is the negative spirit of indifference, which treats all men alike with distant respect, not an intelligent justice, *suum cuique tribuens*. It proceeds almost as much from a want of mental grasp as from the determination to offend nobody'[34].

The antitheses here established between 'a generous suavity of temper' and the distribution of 'equal justice' or between 'fairness' and 'an intelligent justice' are of the utmost importance in understanding the later Acton. He saw no contradiction between first appreciation and then condemnation. Fairness, in the sense of saying in every case the best that might be said in favour of a particular policy or personality, became a reproach. It showed the inability to distinguish between right and wrong, between good and evil. Similarly, Acton's criticism of Ranke's 'dignified isolation' and 'inadequacy of generalisation' was to become the basis of many an attack on the type of impartiality associated with Ranke and his pupils.

What determined the prominence that this side of the young Acton acquired at the expense of the other young Acton who had written: 'Method . . . makes the historian'? The late H. A. L. Fisher found the process 'obscure' by which Acton reached his ultimate categories[35]. Lately, it has been suggested that Acton, 'who had once treated persecution with a certain historical relativity showed an increasingly sensitive nature, as though something in him had been bruised by the spectacles that he had had to witness, whether in the past or in the present'[36]. This may well be the case. It is undoubtedly in accord with the man who would 'impede with microscopic interests the majestic march of civilisation'.

CHAPTER II

The Internal Vision: Sympathy

ACTON's mature mode of thought might be generally introduced with the description of dialectical. He reached his conclusions along a path of thesis and antithesis, of assertion and counter-assertion. The mode of procedure is described in these terms: 'When you perceive a truth, look out for the balancing truth'[1]. Acton's system, using the word with all the reservations imposed by the material, is consequently a closely-knit structure that can be analysed into a number of antithetical propositions of 'truths and balancing truths'. In each case their clash results in raising the argument to a higher level. The structure reaches its culminating point in the negation of history by history. It does not culminate in the present but reaches forward into the future.

The starting point of this ambitious scheme is the recognition that historical knowledge depends on two contrasting modes of vision, and even of experience, each of which has to be allowed full play. 'One must see', Acton writes, 'the inside and the outside of things'[2]. Each mode of vision conceived of history differently and had, accordingly, a different *modus operandi*. Furthermore, since history had this double aspect it followed that either aspect was incomplete without its contrary to balance it. It was only in taking both together that a complete synthesis could be obtained. What Acton understood by seeing and experiencing from the inside is the subject of the present chapter.

He generally used the German word *Romantik* to designate this process. Acton said of his age that it was 'saturated with historic ways of thought'. Jurists had transformed history 'into the likeness of something organic'. Divines had recast their doctrines 'on the lines of development'. Economists had 'dissolved their science into liquid history'. Philosophers had 'bowed the metaphysical neck beneath the historical yoke'[3]. All this was the consequence of the victory of *Romantik*. Acton saw it exemplified in a wide variety of historians, philosophers, political thinkers, novelists and theologians. A typical selection would comprise Burke, de Maistre, Herder, Hegel, Novalis, Tieck, Schlegel, Schleiermacher, Schelling, Döllinger and Savigny[4].

Acton himself was heir to all that was implied in such key-words as 'development' and 'organic'. Probably no movement of his time had a greater influence on him than the romantic movement in its widest sense. To such an extent was this the case that into his own system he incorporated bodily the whole range of romantic presuppositions.

But before considering in detail what *Romantik* meant to Acton, it must first be shown how he dealt with the movement as a historical phenomenon, for the two cannot be separated. What, in other words, was the origin of the Romantic school? Acton believed that its emergence at the turn of the eighteenth and nineteenth centuries was not an accident but rather a function of the contemporary political situation. As a historical phenomenon it formed the 'resistance to the revolutionary rationalism' of the eighteenth century[5]. In his Cambridge Inaugural Lecture of 1895 he described in slightly greater detail 'the mission' of the school (though he did not refer to it by name). It was, he said, 'to make distant times, and especially the Middle Ages... intelligible and acceptable to a society issuing from the eighteenth century'. The romantics, with their notion of development, would explain that there is 'no common code', that moral notions are 'always fluid', that in judging men 'you must consider the times, the class... the surrounding influences, the masters in their schools, the preachers in their pulpits, the movement they obscurely obeyed....' In this way there would henceforth be no 'gratuitous victories' for Voltaire[6]. The past would be rescued from the scorn of the eighteenth-century rationalist. He would easily be convicted of judging the past with the ideas of the present – the prime historical fallacy. The past would be re-established in its own right as a counterweight to the claims of revolution and reason.

Such, for Acton, was the historical or genetic explanation of *Romantik*. But this did not by any means exclude the possibility that the movement, however much itself historically conditioned, might not also contain elements of permanent value. In fact, the very means whereby romanticism fulfilled its role as a historical phenomenon was the basis of Acton's appreciation of the permanent value rendered to history by the movement. In the first place, in order that the movement should indeed rescue the past, it could only do so on something more than an individual scale. Acton himself points out that if it were to explain a man, it would have to take into account that man's class, education, religion. The man did not exist *in vacuo* but he bore within him certain very numerous characteristics of his time and environment, from which he could not be abstracted. Conversely, an artistic movement, for example, could also not be dissociated from its individual exponents.

The past, and, for that matter, the present as well, could not be understood by reference to any single manifestation. Both had to be taken *en bloc*. Thus, one aspect of romanticism that Acton welcomed without qualification was that it brought 'into action the whole inheritance of man. It was attempted *for the first time*'[7]. He expanded on this in another passage of the notes: 'Romantik enlarged the horizon of culture. Everything was brought into it – antiquity, Middle Ages, The East, Literature, Language, Comparative methods in science, Criticism, Philosophy . . .'[8]

In the second place, romanticism had a 'scientific kernel' and this Acton termed 'historicism'. He described it as 'not a phase – but a step, not a hypothesis – but a discovery, not a movement – but an advance'[9]. He usually summed up the substance of this advance in the one word 'sympathy'. This was the attitude of mind that enabled the historian to grasp, or enter into, or experience the past. It is not a concept that Acton can be said to have clarified in any detail but its general purport, which is all that can profitably be discussed, bears a marked resemblance to what Dilthey understood by *Nacherleben*. Acton referred to Dilthey as 'the ripest product of the philosophy of the Continent'[10]. As Acton considered the age to be 'saturated with historic ways of thought' and historicism and historical-mindedness to be the mark of his time[11], his reference to the 'ripeness' of Dilthey was evidently meant to convey that here he saw the culminating point of this nineteenth-century movement. Be that as it may, their terminology, allowing for differences in philosophical background, can be very similar at times. Dilthey wrote, for example: 'The historian cannot renounce the attempt to understand history in terms of itself on the basis of the analysis of the various systems of activity'[12]. Acton's version of this runs: 'It takes long to be really at home in many ages, to feel with them, to limit one's knowledge and adapt one's ideas to their's'[13].

In order to achieve this 'being at home' the exercise of sympathy was required. History is visualised by the sympathetic historian not as a series of facts but as 'a process' which is 'not learnt like grammar or geometry'[14]. The historian divests himself of any views of his own in order that he should not be hampered in his identification of himself with the historical process. He becomes at one with the past. In other words, he re-enacts the past in his own mind, history itself becoming an expression of the reality of mind which the historian is required to re-animate in all its fulness. Hence Acton's emphasis in discussing the romantic task is always placed on the lack of presuppositions and on the corresponding need for emotional absorption. The romantic puts 'imagination and constructiveness before analysis and criticism'; he teaches 'the appreciation of every standpoint' and 'sympathy even with that which repelled'. He judges a man 'by his time, the time by its degree of advancement and knowledge'. He sees 'things *im Werden*', appreciates 'the stages of insight', studies 'the genesis of things'[15].

In this same spirit of universal comprehension, many of Acton's aphorisms demand of the historian that he understand his opponents so much better than they do themselves as to be able to improve their case for them. His remarks go far beyond the conventional desideratum of fairness: 'We estimate a historian very much less by his own ideas than by the justice he does to the ideas which he rejects – not for his national, his religious, his political views, but for his appreciation of nations, religions, parties not his own . . . We never understand a view as long as we think it mean – that is, until we have stripped it of meanness. . . . Not cling to an opinion without knowing all that can be said against it, or reject it without knowing all that can be said in its favour.... Not enough to do justice to a theory. When you see a flaw in an argument, try to improve it'[16].

It would be idle to pretend that Acton's conception of sympathy is founded on any detailed analysis of its possibility. He can, for example, show nothing comparable in this respect to such related thinkers as Dilthey and Collingwood, who also use the 'inside-outside' concepts. But if Acton does not demonstrate by any means the possibility of sympathy, he does at least describe it in action. When he wishes to give a concrete example of his intention he refers to the novelist or playwright – to Victor Hugo, Shakespeare or George Eliot. In a long letter to Mary Gladstone he described what he saw of their varying capacities to see men and matters from the inside. He also spoke of his own endeavours in the same respect: 'My life', he wrote, 'is spent in endless striving to make out the inner point of view, the *raison d'être*, the secret of fascination for powerful minds, of systems of religion and philosophy, and of politics, the offspring of the others, and one finds that the deepest historians know how to display their origin and their defects, but do not know how to think or to feel as men do who live in the grasp of the various systems. And if they sometimes do, it is from a sort of sympathy with the one or the other, which creates partiality and exclusiveness and antipathies. Poets are no better. Hugo, who tries so hard to do justice to the Bishop and Conventionnel, to the nuns and the Jacobinical priest, fails from want of contact with the royalist nobleman and the revolutionary triumvirate, as Shakespeare fails ignobly with the Roman Plebs. George Eliot seemed to me capable not only of reading the diverse hearts of men, but of creeping into their skin, watching the world through their eyes, feeling their latent background of conviction, discerning theory and habit, influences of thought and knowledge, of life and of descent, and having obtained this experience, recovering her independence, stripping off the borrowed shell, and exposing scientifically and indifferently the soul of a Vestal, a Crusader, an Anabaptist, an Inquisitor, a Dervish, a Nihilist, or a Cavalier without attraction, preference or caricature. And each of them should say that she displayed him in his strength, that she gave rational form to motives he had imperfectly analysed, that she laid bare features in his character he had never realised'[17].

At the opposite pole to romantic sympathy stood positivism or rationalism, which in this respect Acton used as well-nigh synonymous terms. He meant thereby the treatment of history as a branch of natural science, as something akin to 'grammar or geometry'. The historian of this school stands apart from his material in a manner reminiscent of the scientist in his laboratory; and, again like the scientist, the historian concerns himself with the discovery of the facts as a preliminary to their organisation into a system of inductive laws. By this means history attains the rank and status of a science with the ability to make predictions, trace patterns and the like, all on the basis of a series of regularly observed phenomena. History, in the positivist's eyes, is conceived of as a series of isolated facts which exist in their own right in a world entirely separate from that of the historian. Mind and nature are two separate entities. The possibility of interaction between them is excluded.

Acton dissents from this position and quotes from Windelband to the effect that positivism, in its extension to historical problems 'must come to grief'[18]. The same condemnation falls on the *Aufklärung*. It was 'directly opposed to history', he writes. It divided men 'into those who lived before Wolff, and themselves'[19]. The burden of this attack is to be found in the charge: 'Rationalism . . . did not teach sympathy'[20]. If rationalism did not teach sympathy, then it could not understand or experience the past. It could not understand the *Zeitgeist*. It could not grasp what made one epoch different from any other. It could not see a man in his totality. Above all, it could not penetrate beneath the surface of an epoch and uncover the process of development and change. It was restricted to seeing in history an unchanging pattern of scientific laws.

'A wrong opinion is never conquered', runs one of Acton's notes, 'until it has reached its most perfect expression. And we are never masters of it until we have seen it at its best'[21]. Acton had seen romanticism at its best and had mastered it. But he had seen it also in its most perfect expression and he now proceeded to conquer it by showing its inadequacy. It was not for nothing that he also quoted Goethe's dictum – the classical is healthy and the romantic sickly[22].

Wherein does the romantic inadequacy show itself? It is characteristic of Acton's thought that the more romanticism became for him a model, the more it exposed itself to attack. The more successful the movement was in its aim of displaying from the inside, the more reprehensible it became in other respects. In fact, it is possible to go even farther. The more romanticism succeeded in its aim of showing in its own light the all and everything of a particular theme or individual, the more it failed; and the cause of its success was at the same time the cause of its failure. The argument brought by Acton against romanticism is that its limitation to the historical level necessarily and inevitably entails the neglect of the non-historical level. It is tantamount to an examination without background or perspective, without any attempt at discrimination. The level of history is by definition identical for all the manifestations of history.

Hence the latter in themselves, all being accorded the same treatment, come to present an identical appearance. Their criterion is the mere brute fact of their existence; and their criterion of differentiation remains merely historical.

This is the reason why Acton found 'historicism' and 'historical-mindedness' to be 'depressing names'[23]. The romantic historian or novelist, such as Acton took George Eliot to be, by treating his subject-matter in its own light, implicitly or explicitly denies that there exists any world other than that expressed in and by the subject-matter itself. His 'appreciation of every standpoint' is equivalent to a vision of the world as limited to any particular standpoint, for the first is unattainable without the second. History conceived in this manner thus shows an infinite number of different worlds, all of which are mutually exclusive. Each exists in its own right and no comment external to it is conceivable. The only conclusion permissible to the historian would be restricted to a note on the manifoldness of possible worlds. It is highly questionable whether Acton's analysis of George Eliot is justified. Assuming it were, however, her Cavalier and her Inquisitor, her Anabaptist and her Dervish would be, when juxtaposed, deprived of their claim to the possession of any absolute validity. In answer to their affirmation of this, the historian would be able to point to the flanking claims. As a result each set of claims would be turned into history, that is, relativised. There would be, on the premisses of the romantic, no possibility of differentiation or discrimination between the Cavalier or the Anabaptist. It has been well said of Dilthey's ultimate position that history itself became 'absolute'[24]. When to this is added the view that the historian himself is *inescapably* subject to the influence of his time the culminating point of historicism is reached – anything that the historian cares to write is history[25].

Acton did not foresee this extreme position, although he did of course grasp the drift towards it. His ultimate rejection of *Romantik* stemmed not from any possible consequence of this kind but rather from its inescapable falsity, *i.e.* although purporting to give, free from any hampering presuppositions, the entire truth of the historical subject, this was precisely what romanticism failed to do. To treat each and every subject in its own light had the consequence of robbing it of its non-historical claims. It was for him a fact that the individual had some experience of a non-historical world to which attention must be given. The romantic, concerned as he was purely with history, could not consider that which was not history. 'If there is no God,' wrote Acton, 'our ideas of good and evil come from experience – the criterion is in the result. Success in the long run determined the right'[26]. In other words, the real, whatever it may be, is also the rational. It is as a result meaningless: a mere datum, for had it not existed the rationality of that which existed in its stead could also not be contested. Its existence would also have placed it in the right. The world of historical experience beyond which the romantic could not pass was inherently irrational. Yet this falsified, for example, the position of the Anabaptist. Did he consider that he might equally well not have existed?

The internal vision of sympathy therefore required to be complemented and corrected by the external vision. The external vision might accept or reject what it saw, but in either case it would be acknowledging a non-historical context. However much the historian who saw from the outside might come to reject the absolute content of the views of an Anabaptist, he would at least be acknowledging their existence in a manner that the romantic was debarred from doing.

The name that Acton gave to the external vision was

morality. It was this that enabled the historian to gauge the rationality of his data. As opposed to the acceptance on principle of the existence of the real, it subjected this existence to the test of rationality. He contrasted the two principles as follows: 'The modern theory of entering into every situation and every system, leads directly up to rehabilitation . . . It ends by excluding the moral standard'[27]. It was precisely on this basis that Acton signified his disagreement with Hegel, the arch-priest of *Romantik*. 'If, with Hegel,' he wrote, 'we considered history as all reason, as the expansion of reason, we should probably be tempted to ignore evil and to deny morality'[28].

CHAPTER III

The External Vision: Morality

FOR the historian, morality has the function of serving as his external vision. How does it do this? In the same way as the concept of sympathy requires the complete absorption of the subject in the object, the concept of morality requires the complete withdrawal of the subject from the object, of the historian from the level of historical experience. His viewpoint is the direct antipode of the romantic. On principle he makes no attempt to sympathise with the object of study but to apply, even mechanically perhaps, the criteria of morality. His attitude is as positivistic as the romantic's is not. He stands apart from his material; he can trace a chain of causation; he can detect laws and patterns. He does not accept but he questions, categorises and concludes. The past is 'there' and the historian 'here'. Between the two spheres no attempt at interaction is made. It is a question of two utterly distinct historical attitudes. In the one case the attitude derives its validity from history itself. In the other the validity is derived from non-history.

What was the content of Acton's morality? On what basis did the external historian question, categorise and conclude? At the centre of Acton's concern lay the position of man. Probably no historian has laid as much stress as did Acton on making man the centre of his attention. If this is not grasped as an overriding principle then it is impossible at all to understand what Acton meant by morality. He made man the measure of all things and the criterion of judgement. Acton was first and foremost a humanist and his morality was such as to illuminate the world from this single viewpoint of the condition of man. This statement must immediately be qualified by two conditions. It would otherwise convey the totally erroneous impression that Acton held both to the innocence of man and to his autonomy. To neither of these propositions did he assent, which in itself is sufficient to distinguish his position from that of the conventional humanist. Acton believed neither in man's essential goodness nor in his capacity to determine his own destiny. His attitude on both counts was complex to a degree. Thus he noted: 'Always expect to find vice and virtue mixed in the character of man, strength and weakness, good and evil in their motives, truth and error in their opinions'[1]. In the notes to the Inaugural he quoted in the same strain the Oxford theologian James Mozley: 'A Christian is bound by his very creed to suspect evil, and cannot release himself . . . He sees it where others do not; his instinct is divinely strengthened; his eye is supernaturally keen; he has a spiritual insight, and senses exercised to discern . . . He owns the doctrine of original sin; that doctrine . . . prepares him for recognising anywhere what he knows to be everywhere'[2]. This view of original sin found expression in Acton's most famous dictum – 'power tends to corrupt and absolute power corrupts absolutely'[3]. This is indeed a frequent theme[4]. It is all the more so in view of Acton's insistence that popular, as distinct from personal power 'may be tainted with the same poison'[5]. He could therefore give but a hesitant welcome to the Reform Bills of the nineteenth century. He described the new electors as 'utterly ignorant', 'unstable' and 'easily deceived by appeals to prejudice and passion'. 'A true Liberal,' he added, 'as distinguished from a Democrat, keeps this peril always before him'[6].

This was one side of the picture. But dark though it was, it did not obscure the other and more hopeful side. If Acton was profoundly pessimistic as to human nature, his pessimism was not so great as to exclude the possibility of optimism. Each qualified the other. The corruptibility of man did not exhaust the potentiality of human nature. At its lowest, for example, it was 'easier to find people fit to govern themselves than people fit to govern others'[7]. At its highest – and here he transcended the theory of the man-centred universe – he spoke of 'the divine image in the soul', of men as brethren, as the children of God, and of conscience as the source of this teaching[8]. Finally, he postulated the interdependence of man and God as the basis of morality: 'The rights of man on earth are the consequence of the rights of God in Heaven'[9].

Let us now go a step further. This relationship between God and man demanded respect for man. Here lay the overriding claim made by Acton's morality upon history. It was because man, despite all his weakness, bore within him some divine element that Acton was a humanist and that the kernel of his morality was respect for man. In his treatment of religion this came strongly to the fore. Christianity for example was 'rather a system of ethics which borrowed its metaphysics elsewhere' than 'a mere system of metaphysics which borrowed some ethics from elsewhere'[10]. In conformity with this he would emphasise those elements in religion which bore a humanist aspect. He termed 'Ethics of Unbelief' the view that 'Christianity (is) chiefly for relations to God'[11]. This represented the extreme of other-worldliness. At the extreme of this-worldliness stood paganism, which took 'the whole of religious duty' to be centred in 'the qualities which relate to life with other men'. Acton sought a balance 'when obligations to man do not interrupt duties to God'[12]. However, if it be true that these are valid criteria, then Acton unquestionably inclined to the pagan extreme. His view of morality was such as to place the utmost stress on the obligations due from man to man and to leave other-worldly considerations in relative abeyance. He wrote to Creighton that in his, Acton's scales, the 'high morality' of Penn the Quaker, outweighed the systems of Barrow, Baxter and Bossuet – although these latter were 'higher, spiritually, constructively, scientifically'[13].

Acton, therefore, judged a man not by his theory but by his practice[14]; and the practice by which he judged was the respect accorded by man to his fellow men. It meant respect for their views – 'wisdom appears less in opinions than in the treatment of other men's'[15] – and it meant respect for their right to existence. *Above all*, it meant respect for their right to existence. This was the touchstone, the infallible guide to the moral standing of a man, a regime or any human institution whatsoever. If the regime respected man, no praise could be higher. If the regime degraded man or took his life, then no greater condemnation could be uttered. 'Our judgment of men, and parties, and systems, is determined by the lowest point they touch. Murder, as the conventional low-water mark, is invaluable as our basis of measurement'. It is the 'scientific zero'[16]. In a letter to Lady Blennerhassett, Acton wrote that only life was 'absolutely essential . . . *c'est la vie humaine qui est l'arche sainte. Personne ne peut être plus décidément caractérisé et condamné que celui qui verse le sang. Cela tranche toute question et contre-balance toute autre chose*'[17]. The centre-piece of morality, as the historian's external viewpoint, is summed up most pithily in one of the 'canons' appended to Acton's letter to Creighton: 'The greatest crime is homicide'[18].

Acton always maintained that his appeal was to 'the common, even the vulgar code', that it implied 'nothing but what was universally current and familiar', that it was without '*découverte nouvelle ou personnelle*'. There is of course a sense in which this was true, a sense that does indeed justify Acton's frequent protestations at those of his friends and contemporaries who accused him of harshness and inhumanity. All would undoubtedly have subscribed to the sanctity of human life with the same forcefulness as did he. Their stand would have been identical. Whence arose, then, the frequent controversies in which his point of view involved Acton?

Although more will be said later in this respect, his differences at different times with Döllinger and Creighton are conclusive. In theory there was of course no difference. This did not emerge until the transition was made to a concrete historical situation – in both cases the Inquisition and the conduct of the medieval popes. Here both Creighton the Protestant and Döllinger the Catholic hedged. When it was necessary to apply to a collective, or to the representatives of a collective, moral criteria they drew back. For Creighton 'anyone engaged in great affairs occupied a representative position, which required special consideration. Selfishness, even wrongdoing, for an idea, an institution, the maintenance of an accepted view of the basis of society, does not cease to be wrongdoing: but it is not quite the same as personal wrongdoing'[19]. For Acton, on the other hand, no 'special consideration' was permissible. For him there had to exist the utmost degree of intimacy between the theory of morality and its practice. His opponents were prepared, even if unwillingly, to allow the collective to pursue its aims in a region removed from morality. This Acton was not prepared to do. To him theory and practice were one. He demanded that public or political life – the two terms are used interchangeably – be yoked to the same moral desiderata in respect of the sanctity of human life. An institution which shed blood incurred the same moral condemnation as did an individual. This was where the unmistakable cleavage arose that divided Acton from his contemporaries of whatever religious or political persuasion.

As a young man his views had been considerably more conventional, for which reason a comparison with their later content is all the more instructive. Acton had then maintained that the things that are God's must be rendered to God, and the things that are Caesar's to Caesar. By avoiding the coincidence of the two sets of obligations, by establishing the separation of the two spheres of authority, absolutism would be rendered impossible. Acton contrasted this favourably with what he termed 'the Jewish and Gentile world': '... in the theocracy of the Jews as in the πολιτέια of the Greeks, the State was absolute. Now it is the great object of the Church, by keeping the two spheres permanently distinct, by rendering to Caesar the things that are Caesar's, and to God the things that are God's, to make all absolutism, of whatever kind, impossible'[20]. This division he later came to reject in favour of a unity that would identify the two sets of claims. He came to deplore the division between temporal and spiritual. The world must be regarded as an indivisible whole, subject in all its aspects to the moral claim. History and morality must be prevented from 'going asunder'[21]. He wrote jocularly to Mary Gladstone: 'Have you not discovered, have I never betrayed, what a narrow doctrinaire I am, under a thin disguise of levity?... Politics come nearer religion with me, a party is more like a church, error more like heresy, prejudice more like sin, than I find it to be with better men'[22].

To complete this theoretical outline of what Acton understood by morality, a qualification, that is at the same time the reverse side to his demand for public integrity, must be added: certain aspects of private life he exempted from moral concern. Here again Acton was contradicting the accepted view and reversing the usual order of precedence. Public behaviour was morally relevant to an overwhelming degree, whereas private behaviour was relatively negligible. 'Chastity not so applicable' runs one cryptic note[23]. Acton admonishes the historian: 'do not so much mind the sins of private life'[24]. Again with a jocular turn, Acton wrote to Lady Blennerhassett that as far as history is concerned the seven deadly sins do not exist. He continued: '*Que Louis XVIII ait été glouton, Pitt ivrogne, Washington colère, Burke peu délicat en affaires, Hamilton peu fidèle en marriage, Fox joueur, Schelling brutal, cela me touche bien peu*'[25]. But all this, it is clear, was merely a question of establishing relative degrees of importance. It was merely a way of showing that in Acton's eyes 'persecution was a crime of a worse order than adultery'; that the actions of Ximenes were 'considerably worse' than the entertainments given by Alexander VI to the courtesans of Rome[26]. If he dispensed private life from judgment, it was only for the purpose of scrutinising all the more closely public life.

Acton baptised his morality with the name of liberalism. He wrote that the 'object' of liberals was 'not political, or national or ecclesiastical, but moral'[27]. This choice of name was most infelicitous, for though there is indeed much common ground between Acton and the liberal, as the term is generally understood, there is also no doubt that in the last resort the two attitudes stood poles apart. This applied as much to a liberal of the stamp of Gladstone as it did to a lesser man such as Morley. There could be no room for the co-existence of Acton's uncompromising liberalism based on an absolute certitude of the knowledge of right and wrong with what had to become in effect the live-and-let-live attitude of either Parliamentarian. The case was identical in the narrower field of history. Liberalism, or morality, could not admit of compromise with *Romantik*.

As is so often the case with Acton, his view is posited in the form 'either - or'. Either God exists – or experience teaches 'the ideas of good and evil'. Either every situation and system is 'rehabilitated' – or 'the moral standard' is retained. Again, when reviewing Sir Erskine May's *Democracy in Europe*, he wrote: 'If nothing was certain in theology, there was no certainty in ethics and no moral obligation'. If the will of God was not 'the rule of life', then 'every man and every body of men had the right to do what they had the means of doing'[28]. For Acton it was a case of all – or nothing.

The romantic and the liberal balanced each other, but they might not be confounded with each other. One was historical, the other extra-historical. The one viewed from the inside, the other from the outside. The ideal historian amalgamated both approaches so as to comprehend history both in its own light and in the light of that which was not history. He sympathised both with everything and with nothing.

What Acton understood by morality has so far been discussed virtually in a vacuum, far removed from that very sphere of history where its relevance was paramount. This would be an inadequate procedure in the best of circumstances. But in Acton's case, where morality bore so overwhelmingly on conduct, and especially public and political conduct, this procedure requires more than ever to be transposed from the theoretical to the historical. A morality that all but eschews theoretical justification to concentrate all the more on practical manifestations must necessarily suffer disproportionately when it is deprived of the contact with reality. Not only would it be true to say that such a contact is essential in order to endow morality with a living content. It would also be necessary to show how Acton made, or rather attempted to make, his view of morality the concern of the collective and not merely of the individual.

Furthermore, such a contact or confrontation, shows that Acton's morality, however uncompromising in principle, could not absolutely withstand the complexities of reality. His intent was of course to demonstrate the absoluteness of the moral claim. There were times, indeed, when he spoke as though it might be possible to tot-up moral behaviour by the 'statistical method' rather than the historical. The former 'gave a more exact induction'[29]. But if this be classified as a temporary aberration, it could still not be claimed that he succeeded in maintaining the external vision in all its purity. Sometimes he had, much against the grain, to concede ground to the internal vision; sometimes, for example, the man who shed blood was not always a murderer. If Acton spoke of 'the inflexible integrity of the moral code', he could also speak of 'the wavy line between religion and politics'[30]. For all these reasons, then, Acton's morality must be shown in practice.

The choice of examples might be made from virtually any of the different aspects of reality with which Acton dealt as a historian. But of this *embarras de richesse* the three most suitable aspects are Acton's dispute with Döllinger on moral judgements and religious persecution, his view of Parliamentary government in Victorian England, and his view of Christianity. None of these subjects is self-contained. Each overlaps into the others, all the more so as Acton sought in each case the general and not the particular. Nevertheless, each possesses in itself sufficient unity to serve as a focus of attention.

*

Taking each in turn, the controversy with Döllinger dated back to 1879 when Lady Blennerhassett published in the *Nineteenth Century* an article in general praise of Dupanloup, Bishop of Orleans at the time of his death the previous year. The article was prefaced by a note from Döllinger extolling Dupanloup's virtues as a Christian prelate. It was this that Acton found sufficiently provocative to touch off a basic dispute with his respected teacher. The striking feature of the tribute was its contrast with Dupanloup's past role as a defender of the Syllabus of 1864 and his attitude to the Infallibility Dogma. He had not opposed it in principle but had considered its proclamation to be inopportune. In 1870 Dupanloup was to be found amongst the leaders of the Inopportunist party. On both scores, of course, he was in opposition to Acton and Döllinger.

But that the latter two were also not at one now became apparent. Acton reacted immediately and unfavourably to Döllinger's note: he found it lacking in the requisite moral fervour. At the personal level, perhaps, Acton was not the man to tax Döllinger with moral laxity. The former had preferred a more than ambiguous relationship to the Church rather than follow the heedings of conscience. The latter, on the other hand, had chosen excommunication in preference to the acceptance of a dogma in which he could not wholly believe. But this personal element must be disregarded if the conflict is to receive the attention it merits. What began as a dispute over the propriety of praising Dupanloup rapidly broadened out into the issue of religious and political persecution, as evidenced, for example, in the Inquisition or the Massacre of St Bartholomew. Between the two men there grew up 'a gulf almost too wide for sympathy'[31].

For Döllinger persecution was an 'evil'; for Acton a 'crime'[32]. What lay behind this terminology? Döllinger's position was simplicity itself. He was, Acton noted, 'very much against tyranny. But that does not make a liberal'[33]. And the reason why Döllinger did not make a liberal, in Acton's sense of the term, was his historical-mindedness. His 'foremost maxim' was 'to look at things historically'. He always 'saw things in their own light – applying their own canons'[34]. Consequently, when Döllinger looked at the Inquisition, he saw it, however much he might deplore the institution, not primarily from the viewpoint of moral disapproval. He saw it rather in its historical context. There were, he said, 'arguments of time, surroundings, education, authority, ignorance'[35]. Döllinger would not only allow for these extenuating circumstances. He would place them in the forefront of his picture. He told Acton that nothing had varied so much as the guilt imputed to homicide. There was the vendetta and lynch law.... There was the accomplice who got a price for head-money....[36] The principle of the Inquisition, Döllinger implied, might certainly be reprehensible but he could not dissociate it from the spirit of the time. If he applied to it the Inquisition's own canons, as Acton accused him of doing, then, indeed, he could understand – even though he might continue to disapprove. The Inquisitors themselves had no awareness of wrongdoing. Moreover, Döllinger asked, had he been born several centuries earlier, who knew but that he too might have been found amongst them[37]. How, therefore, could he arrogate to himself the right to condemn others for what he himself, but for an accident of time, might so easily have perpetrated?

Behind the gentle and scholarly Munich professor of the nineteenth century there lurked an Inquisitor of the thirteenth. Döllinger did not condone the Inquisitors, but he also did not condemn them.

That Acton himself could appreciate the force of this argument is clear from his treatment of, for example, the Massacre of St Bartholomew. He could be no less historically-minded than Döllinger. If the latter could explain and justify the Inquisition on the basis of 'time, surroundings, education, authority, ignorance' then Acton could apply the same method to St Bartholomew. He could and did describe the association of the Huguenots with 'vast political interests'; he could refer to their own intolerance, to the struggle in France between themselves and the Catholics, to the ramification throughout Europe of internal French politics[38]. All this, and much more besides, would constitute the socio-historical context. As such, it would explain the origin of the massacre. It would show why and how it happened, the background and the motives. But – and this is the significant point – it would show nothing more. Data drawn from reality could not supply their own criterion of moral justification. If it were shown, as it easily could be, how a certain episode arose from a certain background, then the result might just as well be to condemn the background as to condone the episode.

Acton would never admit in principle that a sort of 'half-way house' might be erected at the head of two paths – one marked condemnation and the other condonation. It was essential that one or the other path be taken. 'In questions of life and death', he wrote, 'there must be a decision. Both cannot be right'[39]. Much might be said for and against, but in the last resort an unambiguous answer must be given. At the end of a lengthy examination there must stand a conclusion and not a question-mark. In principle, there could not be 'two courts of final appeal'. Acton ironically compared a writer who 'did not care for the inquisitor' but who 'would not resist him in the discharge of his duty' with 'a traveller who discovered a precipice to the right of him, another to the left, and nothing between'[40]. This was where Döllinger stood – or rather failed to stand.

What was the basis of Acton's counter-argument? Why did he write to Mary Gladstone that the principle of the Inquisition was 'murderous', that a man's opinion of the Papacy was 'regulated and determined by his opinion about religious assassination'?[41]. Acton's reply bore, to begin with, upon a refutation of the personal viewpoint alleged by Döllinger. The moral law, he said in the Inaugural, 'is written on the tablets of eternity'[42]. Even though it might be man himself who made the moral law articulate, this did not gainsay its existence independent of man. The law might speak with the voice of man but its utterance owed nothing, or virtually nothing, to the spokesman. If the source of morality was eternity, as Acton asserted, then the judgment lacked all personal aspect, *i.e.* it was not a case where one fallible individual stood in judgment over another. It was a case where man was judged from an external standpoint by standards drawn from an ideal conception of human conduct. Morality, through the historian, judged man by the standard of conduct that he should attain and not by that actually attained.

It could not indeed do otherwise. No alternative was logically at all conceivable. Acton had little difficulty in putting his finger on the flaw in Döllinger's reasoning. Reviewing George Eliot's life, by J. W. Cross, he wrote that she could 'neither be defended on the plea that every man must be tried by canons he assents to, nor censured on the plea that virtue consists in constant submission to variable opinion. The first would absolve fanatics and the other would supersede conscience'[43]. Were either course attempted, were a man judged either according to his own lights or the lights of his time, then the path would be cleared to the permissibility of whatever might happen. No world external to man or his society would exist, whence judgment might be possible. What man has not absolved himself for his actions? Of what society has the 'variable opinion' not given its imprimatur, by its very nature, to the most varied actions? Neither, therefore, could supply the unchanging standard that was required, were morality not to be deprived of all meaning.

Furthermore, Acton also had no difficulty in showing that a reasoning such as Döllinger's would lead to absurdity. When followed to its inescapable conclusion, it would amount to saying of a situation that it arose through no man's fault, that though it was man-made, no man would bear the responsibility. There would be, as Acton put it, 'crime without a culprit, the unavenged victim who perishes by no man's fault, law without responsibility, the virtuous agent of a vicious cause . . .'[44]. If there were victims, then there must be guilt and injustice. And it was because Acton saw from the standpoint of the victims, that he was unable to acquit the guilty of their crime. If a human life with all its divine content and reflection had been desecrated, then it was no help to justify the desecrators on the grounds of their ignorance or education.

It seems that in 1882 the dispute with Döllinger came to a head. On 16th July of that year Acton drafted a document headed *Notes on an Important Conversation* in which he crystallised his position. It is all the more important in that it indicated some at least of the cases where his morality might compromise with time. That Acton was in principle an advocate of an absolute moral standard must not lead to the conclusion that absolute standards could or should be applied to human conduct as if they were a mechanical measuring-rod. In moments of exasperation he certainly said that he could make no allowance for any human weakness whatsoever. But in more considered and measured moments it was of 'a wavy line' and not 'an inflexible integrity' that he spoke. The crucial point is where he placed the emphasis – and here there is of course not the slightest doubt. The main body of the document runs: '... I thought that Bossuet and Arnauld cannot be spoken of as pious and religious men seeing their attitude towards the Revocation [of the Edict of Nantes] and other things, but that they are a dishonour to the Church. I wished to judge by manifest canons and not by sympathy; to apply the canons equitably, to friend and foe, leaving no room for favour, or privilege, or prejudice. For I observed that everybody is determined by likes and dislikes, by something in his own wishes and experience, and all this I knew must be shut out of conscientious history. Therefore I somewhat dreaded the arbitrary margin of extenuating circumstances and qualified guilt. Murder, being, in the view of society, the worst of crimes, seemed the most decisive test of character. Apart from self-defence, or what is equivalent to self-defence, as in the case of Charlotte Corday and of the men who slew Conrad of Marburg, a murderer seemed to me good for nothing but hanging. To admit excuses and pleas in mitigation of so great a crime, is to open the door to all manner of partiality. I do not know how to differentiate Carnot and Danton... Guy Fawkes and Napoleon. As I know nothing more infamous than murder, the worst of these appears to me not more infamous than the best. Because St Just was also a thief, and Borromeo a hero of devotion, I dare not think worse of the one or better of the other. The glare of the sun extinguishes all other lights. I have no instruments delicate enough to detect the stars at noon. If, for the purposes of history, murder is the worst of crimes, those who promote it or defend it, before or after, share in proportion the guilt of the culprit. And I feel that my hands are cleaner, that I am on the safer side, if I commit all such to the execration and vengeance of man. . . . Ximenes seems to me worse than his victims.

I do not exclude all circumstances or all consideration of date. As long, for instance, as private war flourished and it was every man's business to kill an outlaw, the killing of heretics is not quite what it afterwards became. In all these things the judgement is more severe as light and civilisation increase.

The historic spirit which demands indulgence for the thirteenth century requires a stricter code for the nineteenth, a code more strict in proportion to opportunities of religious knowledge and divine grace. In obedience to that law, I am more strict in applying the moral test to contemporaries, especially to educated persons, more to Catholics than to others, still more to priests than to laymen, to prelates most of all'[45]. This was Acton's last word on the subject.

*

The moralist's external view of parliamentary government in England, in the second half of the nineteenth century was again based, by definition, on non-historical criteria. Victorian democracy, a contemporary phenomenon, had to confront the same test as had the Inquisition, a phenomenon of the past. To Acton both came within the same sphere of public life. Both had therefore to satisfy the same moral requirements. Neither could be exempted from this concern. He referred with approval to the 'Hebrew nation' and its 'principle that *all* political authorities must be tested and reformed according to a code which was not made by man'[46].

How did Victorian democracy emerge from this test? Fundamental to Acton's criticism was once again a view of politics subordinated to morality. The *fons et origo* of his criticism, the source whence all the rest emanates is what he calls, in terms reminiscent of Berdyaev, 'the democratic immorality'. He adds that it was 'founded on the absence of any criterion of right and wrong'[47]. In other words, the democratic state did not exist as a means to the fulfilment of the moral aim. It existed devoid of any transcendental purpose whatsoever. It acted purely and simply in response to the demands made on it by those in the best position to make their demands effectively felt. The criterion of right and wrong was left in abeyance. For the same reason, such an associated idea of democracy as '*vox populi vox dei*' was usually regarded by Acton with aversion. In one note he includes it with such other aversions as 'whatever is, is right; heroes above morality; worship of success'[48]. There could be no guarantee that the voice of the people could be any more the voice of morality than the voice of any other group.

With this basic immorality established, Acton went on to trace its active presence in the working of the system. He made it responsible for his most weighty specific charge against Victorian political thinking – its toleration of a double standard of morality. Acton deplored the absence of a 'code of political morality distinct from or beyond the limits of private'. This had as result that political questions could only be treated 'experimentally, by the Baconian methods'[49].

This separation was not only in itself immoral, removing, as it did, by far the larger part of human affairs from moral purview, but it also had as ineluctable consequence the positive encouragement of immorality. It created a region exposed to 'Baconian methods', where anti-moral tendencies could have free play, precisely because it was there that they had taken refuge from the moral claim. A lengthy quotation from the passage just referred to shows Acton's analysis of the situation. It was made in 1887. 'The great bulk of cultured men in our day do not believe that politics are a branch of Moral Science. They think that politics teach what is likely to do good or harm, not what is right and wrong, innocent and sinful. If I say: "I owe this man half-a-crown. He is sure to get drunk on it; shall I pay him?" They will answer – Certainly; you must do your duty, in private life, and wherever the plain rules of morality or the applicable laws extend, regardless of consequences. But they would not admit a like obligation in politics. America cannot be taxed because it is not represented. Civil disabilities for religion must be abolished. Slavery must be put down. The tyranny of Indian princes must be repressed, etc, etc, etc. Such propositions they would deny absolutely. They would say: "It is highly desirable – not obligatory. We must consider consequences, balance probabilities, estimate forces, choose the lesser evil. Until it can be shown that oppression, repression, suppression, damage the interests of the State, there is no good reason to interfere with them. If the State would be greater, stronger, richer, by keeping down part of its subjects, by denying education, by restraining labour, by working children to death in factories, by wars for prestige, etc, etc, etc, then those things are lawful by the only test known to politics. . . .

Thus Maine, Stephen, Dilke, all men who live in diplomacy, all men concerned with India, all men belonging to the Services. Above all, this is part of the teaching of Burke, and from him Morley has adopted it'[50].

Given this distinction of principle, its nefarious influence could be noted in all the institutions of party government. These could be no better than the spirit that they expressed. Acton said of the Cabinet, for example, that its 'solidarity' and 'partnership' required a sort of polite hypocrisy and conspiracy: 'obliges men to defend in public what they condemn in private and to make no secret of their real sentiments to their opponents. It is too well understood'[51]. Furthermore, the Cabinet depended on obtaining a majority and this in turn opened the door to further corruption: 'some weak men will be attracted by what government has to give.... Not mere money.... Patronage'[52]. Acton, finally, summed up 'demoralising debates' with a striking epigram: 'Hansard comes between Boccaccio and Brantôme'[53].

He was, on the other hand, nothing if not realistic. Side by side with denunciations of party government can be found the verdict that it was the 'most moral of all'. The reason that he gives is highly characteristic. It was not because party government was more efficient or more representative. Rather, it tended to develop a spirit of mutual forbearance and tolerance. 'Teaches to treat the opponent to the same rights you claim yourself'[54].

It would give an incomplete picture of Acton's criticism of Victorian democracy were this to be limited to the institutional level alone. Such a criticism requires to be supplemented by the degree to which the system fulfilled Acton's repeated demand that 'liberty was the highest political end'. To do this requires in its turn some mention of his views on economics and socialism. Economics was for Acton an ethical science[55]. He does not expand this but it may reasonably be conjectured to mean a view of economics as concerned with the relations between man and man. It was in accordance with this view that Acton wrote: 'Errors of statesmen – they see not masses of struggling and suffering men, but a force tending outwards'[56]. Acton, however, was not a statesman, and saw what they did not see. He had ever present to his mind the masses of struggling and suffering men.

It was this awareness that determined his insight into the conditions of the poor of his time. A comparison here with Marx is highly apt, and, indeed inevitable, however remote are the two contemporaries in other respects. Acton was anything but a socialist and a thread linking his early and mature views is the hostility to socialism. It was evidently connected in his mind with a complex of ideas embracing nationalism, militarism, and democracy[57]. Even so, Acton thoroughly appreciated the conditions against which socialism represented a protest. The notes contain numerous extracts of this order: 'It is a very common practice with the great populous parishes of London to bind children in large numbers to the proprietors of cotton mills in Lancashire and Yorkshire, at a distance of two hundred miles. The children, who are sent off by wagon-loads at a time, are as much lost for ever to their parents as if they were shipped off for the West Indies'[58]. Acton drew from this situation much the same conclusion as did Marx. (Whether he came to it independently or under the influence of Marx is an open question.) There was for Acton a 'law by which power follows property'[59]. Consequently, since the worker had no property he had no power. He was exposed without defence to the exploiting power of capital. In other words, Acton made the familiar distinction between formal and actual power, formal and actual equality. 'If', he wrote, 'there is a free contract, in open market, between capital and labour, it cannot be right that one of the two contracting parties should have the making of the laws, the management of the conditions, the keeping of the peace, the administration of justice, the distribution of taxes, the control of expenditure, in its own hands exclusively.... Justice required that property should – not abdicate – but – share its political supremacy. Without this partition, free contract was as illusory as a fair duel in which one man supplies seconds, arms and ammunition'[60].

The next step in this analysis pointed to the unsatisfactory nature of any merely political gains that the poor might achieve. 'What the speechless masses of the poor need is not political privileges which they cannot enjoy but comfort – without which political influence is a mockery or a snare'[61].

But none of this made Acton into a socialist or a democrat. Though he acknowledged that the workers' efforts had not been entirely in vain, he did not disguise from himself the price that had been paid: a price which would annihilate the gains achieved. The nett achievement would therefore be to leave man in the same position as before, perhaps, even, in a worse position. What he would gain on the roundabouts, he might more than lose on the swings. In the case of democracy and the old order Acton had no doubt that this would apply.

As a general and abstract principle in his conception of the moral state Acton believed in what he called 'a mixed constitution'. This would 'ensure integrity and capacity in the rulers by popular election, in order that the whole nation may have a share in controlling the government under which it lives, all offices being accessible to merit, all men being electors, and all men being equal in those rights which come not from civilisation but from nature, by reason of the divine image in the soul'[62]. But this principle belonged to the ideal world, and although it was for Acton of the most urgent moment that the ideal should be made real, he did not for that reason conclude that what held good for the one would necessarily be applicable in the other[63].

The argument that Acton brought against democracy or

socialism – he used the two terms well-nigh interchangeably – is reducible to the question of power. The power of capital existed as a fact. If socialism were to overthrow that power, it would necessarily and inescapably have to represent an even greater power. Thus – 'socialism easily accepts despotism. It requires the strongest exertion of power – power sufficient to interfere with property'[64]. What would happen, in fact, is that democracy would unify the power on whose division liberty depended[65]. It represented a form of 'government by idea [which] tends to take in everything, to make the whole of society obedient to the idea. Spaces not so governed are unconquered, beyond the border – unconverted, unconvinced – a future danger'[66].

Acton saw this as the product of popular participation in government. He had written in an early article on Cavour, that the greater the number of people who share in the authority of government, the more that authority will be rendered 'irresistible'[67]. To counterbalance this, of course, the remedy was the existence of as many intermediate powers as possible – government by ideas, and not idea. This remained his hope in later years, but it was a hope qualified by much fear. He had a clear perception of a state where nothing would block the supremacy of the popular will, where the functions assumed by the state in response to the demands of the masses would override all opposition. 'It is bad to be oppressed by a minority, but it is worse to be oppressed by a majority . . . from the absolute will of an entire people there is no appeal, no redemption, no refuge but treason'[68].

Acton's position in relationship to universal education is a useful example of his attitude to what was at the time a novel area of state power. He welcomed it in principle, as he welcomed all efforts at raising the standard of living of the poor. But he also believed control over education to be too tempting to a democratic government. It would inevitably result in the abuse of the power entrusted. 'A government,' he wrote, 'entirely dependent on opinion, looks for some security what that opinion shall be, strives for the control of the forces that shape it, and is fearful of suffering people to be educated in sentiments hostile to its institutions'[69].

It was not of course from socialism or democracy exclusively that Acton anticipated danger. There could be no grosser misrepresentation of his analysis than to present him as an advocate of the old régime. But what he does argue is that whilst democracy, equally with monarch and aristocracy, 'sacrifices everything to maintain itself', it has in addition 'an energy and a plausibility that kings and nobles cannot attain, to override representation . . . and to secure, by Plebiscite, Referendum, or Census, free play for the will of the majority'[70].

Acton's whole vision of the future was naturally heavily darkened by what he saw in the present. In one note he wrote: 'To reconcile liberty with an aristocratical society and a monarchical state was the problem, the striving of many centuries. To preserve it under absolute democracy is the special problem of the future'[71]. In another note he strongly suggests that he had little confidence in the solution of this problem. The note is headed: 'The End: Our dangers'. Beneath stands a short list: 'Omnipotence of Parliament, great military monarchies, Absolutism of the People, Governments will do more and more'[72]. If liberty was the highest political end, as Acton repeatedly asserted, then democracy would push it further and further into the future. The best of intentions would produce the worst of results.

*

Acton's relationship, both to Christianity and to the Church, was ambiguous and ambivalent. This was inevitably the case for, in his own words, it depended on 'a permanent compromise'[73]. There are obvious limits beyond which it is impossible to disentangle the elements of this compromise. Nor is it altogether necessary for the present purpose that these be laid bare in their entirety. Even so, some attempt should be made in order to distinguish as far as possible between Acton's arguments of substance and those of a merely personal nature, thereby allowing his distinctive criticism of Christianity to emerge.

The compromise of which Acton spoke originated in the dual antagonistic elements of Catholicism and Liberalism. His aim was to reconcile them. He wrote in substantially the same terms both to Lady Blennerhassett and to Bishop Creighton. To the former he said that his was 'the story of a man who had started in life believing himself a sincere Catholic and a sincere Liberal; who therefore renounced everything in Catholicism which was not compatible with liberty, and everything in Politics which was not compatible with Catholicity'[74]. To Creighton the same synthesis was displayed: 'It is a real comfort to know that you suffer from my complaint of not getting people to agree with you. . . . I find that people disagree with me either because they hold that Liberalism is not true, or that Catholicism is not true, or that both cannot be true together. If I could find anyone who is not included in these categories, I fancy we should get on very well together'[75].

But what does this mean in actual practice? Is it convincing? Acton once wrote: 'Christianity without liberality will not take us far towards heaven'[76]. This is hardly a satisfactory synthesis for it clearly conflicts with the all-embracing intention of both sets of claims. If Liberalism was an all-embracing creed and even 'a philosophy of history'[77], then it could only be combined with anything else at the expense of its outstanding characteristic, *i.e.* its all-embracing nature. The same applied of course to Catholicism. Neither could embrace any extraneous element at any other price than the sacrifice of its own distinctiveness.

This, at least, was the mode wherein the problem presented itself to Acton. However eclectic he might be, and however widespread the sources whence he drew his ideas, in the last resort – and this is the only resort with which Acton was concerned – there could not be room for two viewpoints, each of which had total claims.

Yet in relation to the Church, this was precisely what he attempted. Acton was trying to ride two horses at the same time. He was trying to be both a Liberal and a Catholic. This comes most clearly to the fore when his attitude towards Catholic persecution is examined. As shown above, his condemnation derived from a view of morality which stressed, to the virtual exclusion of all else, the kind of conduct pursued, making no allowance for good intention or error. But if Acton wrote: 'Rome must stand or fall by the dogma of persecution'[78], he also wrote that the *sine qua non* of 'scientific' thought was the separation between the idea and its exponent[79]. Here Acton made the familiar distinction between the Church as a divine institution and her possibly sinful agents. A complete separation might divide the one from the other. But in the first case no such separation was posited. The Church herself stood condemned by reason of the utterances of her agents. If Rome urged persecution, Rome fell.

Both these positions may be held, of course. But it is not possible to hold both simultaneously as Acton tried to do. Both criteria could not be brought simultaneously into operation, given Acton's view of morality. If this required of him that he judge by conduct then other considerations were irrelevant, or almost so. This was of course the overwhelming emphasis – 'the final judgment depends on the worst *action*'[80]. The fact that this judgment was not applied unambiguously in the case of the Church gives the measure of Acton's ambivalency and compromise.

So much for the personal aspect. However, an argument, Acton writes, must be 'disentangled from the motives and personal ways of men'[81]. Only then can it be appreciated for what it may or may not be worth. What emerges when this 'disentanglement' has taken place? What does Acton's criticism of Christianity amount to, when the personal factors are removed? Finally, and most important, what is the relation of this criticism to morality?

As this last question suggests, Acton did not identify Christianity and morality. Despite everything that the latter owed to the former – and most obviously in the emphasis given to the respect due between man and man – the two visions were not co-terminous. Acton defined Christianity as 'rather a system of ethics which borrowed its metaphysics elsewhere'[82]. It was accordingly the ethical teachings and influence of Christianity that were of primary if not exclusive concern in his evaluation.

In 1890 at Tegernsee Acton dictated to one of his children some notes that the child entitled 'Conversations on Church History held with my father at Tegernsee – Summer 1890'. Acton is there reported to have said that the teaching of the New Testament was 'narrow, simple and limited' and that it was not 'the limit or boundary, but the germ and origin of the Catholic Church'[83]. This criticism refers to the limitation of Christian ethics to the individual sphere and the obligation to extend the same requirements to the public sphere of the collective[84]. For at its broadest the argument brought by

Acton against Christianity stemmed from a view that embraced the whole of life and subjected the whole to the moral on the basis of a single code of behaviour. When Acton wrote, for example, that politics or economics were of moral concern, he did not so much mean that the spiritual should prevail over the temporal but rather that the same code of behaviour was valid for both. Both spheres required to be assimilated to the same norm. This may be taken further to suggest the elimination of any difference in the two spheres. The spiritual was temporal and the temporal spiritual. To join together morality and history meant no less than this. Similarly, when Acton wrote that if a religion 'goes wrong' about morality, it will also 'go wrong' about politics[85], the same identification is indicated.

He considered the moral purview of Christianity too narrow with the consequence that those areas of life with which it did not concern itself might well fall under non-religious influence. On this basis he thought a non-religious system possible, or perhaps that each area of life might develop its own code. He wrote for example to Mary Gladstone: 'There is a very strong tendency to substitute for a religious system another system of obligations, equally determined and absolute, but not at all religious. Especially nowadays when unbelief in the shape of doubt is yielding to unbelief in the shape of certain conviction.

And in these things the influence of religion is by no means certain. It has often been opposed to the theory of the divine right of man. As the history of persecution, of slavery, shows, quite naturally. The New Testament, which deals so largely with private morality, deals very little with public, and introduced only one political idea beyond the Hellenic horizon. If, therefore, we admit the authority of a binding system, independent of religion, we raise up a rival power, in morals as in science. Our conduct becomes subject to a law which is not that of the Church which may deviate from it, and which, at certain points, inevitably collides with it. We live under a divided reign. Christianity becomes an influence instead of an authority, a prop, but not a sufficient guide. The surrender of one bit of its domain to the mathematicians, of another to the economists, of a third to the politicians, may be followed by further encroachment from biologists, evolutionists, and Monistic philosophers.

This is the line of reasoning which makes religious belief a weak security for political principle, unless the faith of men is thoroughly sincere, and even men thoroughly sincere may object that they know not which political theory or which system of the Rights of Man is so surely the right one that, where it commands, they must prefer it to their religion. No consensus, no Vincentian Rule, exists that can decide this question.

Therefore, although I fully admit that political Rights proceed directly from religious duties, and hold this to be the true basis of Liberalism, I do not mean to say that there is no other foundation for a system of right for men who know of no relations between man and God'[86].

This was what might happen in the best of cases. A non-religious system of morality might develop, in such a way as to cover the areas left untouched by Christianity. Earlier in the letter just quoted, Acton mentioned Morellet and Bentham (for Criminal Law), and Jefferson, Lafayette and Sièyes (for the Rights of Man) as examples of unbelievers who had in their different ways attempted this. This was what might happen in the best of cases – even though Acton's praise of Jefferson or Bentham was anything but unqualified. But what might happen in the worst of cases? Acton replied: 'Religion alone is no safeguard for morality. Classical philosophy giving an independent morality, prevents men from falling under such teachers as Knox, Beza, Suarez'[87]. In other words, not even men so 'thoroughly sincere' as Knox, Beza or Suarez knew which system of the 'Rights of Man' to choose. Their religion, despite the intensity of their conviction, gave them little guide in this political question. That this was not accidental, in Acton's view, flows from his fundamental criticism of the Christian attitude towards the world. The failure of Christianity as a public influence formed the complement to the immorality of public life.

He deplored the fact that 'Christianity taught so little politics' and that it was 'so long' before the Fathers of the Church wrote ethics[88]. Conversely, he wrote that 'if the Church was to sanctify Society, it must extend its influence over the State. That private life should be holy, and public life unregenerate, that a citizen should put aside his religion as soon as he accepts political office was out of the question'[89].

In diverse ways Acton traced the roots of this distinction back to the apathy and political disinterestedness of the early Church. 'The Roman Christians', he wrote, '. . . did not dream of controlling the State. They obeyed, or submitted, without resistance. They looked up to power with excessive awe. They allowed it to legislate against Christianity, to make laws for religion, to control the Church. . . . So far from proposing new things, they abstained from public service'[90]. In other passages precisely the same note is struck. Under the heading 'Early Christianity' Acton writes: 'No idea of Christian government. Apparently no expectation of a state of things beyond the pagan empire of Rome. . . . They were taught how to suffer and obey. They had to learn how to govern'[91]. Again, Acton complained that the early Christians 'turned away from the State. Their thoughts in a Kingdom not of this world. Above all, no political party.

Could not convert the Empire. Not at all agreed as to social principles. Some defended slavery; some opposed it. . . .'[92]

The subsequent history of the Church was interpreted in the light of this analysis. Thus, Acton maintained, the conversion of the Roman Empire under Constantine was largely a nominal victory. It could not be held equivalent to the 'sanctification of society' that he demanded. In his lecture, *The History of Freedom in Christianity*, he alleged that *in fact* 'even in the fervent age of its conversion' the Roman Empire made the Church into 'a gilded crutch of absolutism'[93]. What held good in the early history of the Church held good later, even though, as Acton later asserted in the same lecture, liberty emerged as a by-product from the struggle between Church and State. In general terms, interpreting the later as a consequence of the earlier, Acton quoted as an argument against Christianity that 'for the purpose of maintaining itself' it had been 'compatible with tyranny, persecution, torture, slavery, extermination'[94].

The attempt has now been made to measure against morality: firstly, certain historical phenomena; secondly, Victorian democracy, and thirdly, Christianity. In all three aspects the salient features of morality showed themselves to be humanist, non-historical and all-embracing. Acton counselled the historian – 'Resist your time – take a foothold outside it'[95]. This was the balancing-truth to the romantic attitude of identification with time. The historian must similarly balance. He must stand with one foot in the flow of the historical process. With the other he must stand in the unchanging non-historical world – 'aloof with Archimedes'[96]. The first stance enables him to understand and sympathise, and the second to judge. What is seen from this dual vantage-point?

CHAPTER IV

The Contemporaneity of History

To the romantic historian who identifies himself with time and history, the world appears as an infinity of diversities. His material presents him with any number of different historical situations, personalities, systems, institutions and the like. There are no parallels, repetitions or resemblances. Each of the situations that confronts him is unique, and the more he succeeds in conveying this unique character, the greater his achievement as a historian. In the eternal flux of time, without beginning and without end, there are no fixed points; there are only changes. And each of the changes is different from every other change. The only constant that the vision of the romantic equips him to discern is the constant of change itself.

The liberal historian sees of course the same 'material' as the romantic. But because he is standing 'aloof', limiting his angle of vision to the condition of man, the material connotes something entirely different. The view of the romantic appears erroneous and illusory. The liberal sees that in the morally most important respect of all – the treatment of man by man – it is not change but constancy that confronts him. The condition of man is the one constant, the one fixed point in the eternal flux and change. It is not so much that the romantic's identification of change is contradicted by the liberal's identification of constancy but rather that it is overcome and subsumed in a wider synthesis. Both are valid but both require to lose their extreme characteristics before they may be amalgamated into one all-embracing vision capable of doing justice to the two aspects of human existence – that which changes, and that which remains constant. What emerges from this synthesis, from the overcoming of the romantic by the liberal is the transformation of all history into contemporary history.

This can be further explored and illuminated in Acton's relationship to the attacks made by Schopenhauer on Hegel. The virtual victory of Hegelian ideas, in one form or another, during the nineteenth century – a victory of which no one probably was more sensible than Acton himself – has to some extent obscured the significance of such of Hegel's opponents as Kierkegaard, Burckhardt and Schopenhauer. The first-named seems to have left no mark on Acton, although, through a German translation, he was familiar with at least some of Kierkegaard's works. As far as Burckhardt was concerned, Acton knew only the *Kulturhistoriker* and not the author of the *Weltgeschichtliche Betrachtungen.* (These were not published until after Acton's death.) Schopenhauer, on the other hand, came into a different category in so far at least as Acton was thoroughly familiar with all his works. He makes no detailed criticism but his general attitude of approval – if not respect – is clear from his echoing of Schopenhauer's attack on the 'illusory' nature of history. It records, says Acton, 'that which is always the same'[1].

Acton could consequently have little but scorn for the Hegelian conception of progress. Hegel saw in history the unfolding manifestation of reason which would culminate ultimately in the reign of the absolute. This constituted the path of progress through every aspect of change, including violence, revolution and conflict. Acton's specific objection to this scheme of things bore on its evasiveness and artificial harmony. It avoided the problem of evil and produced concord from dissonance. It was an arch-romantic scheme in that it justified all and every change. Hegel, in Acton's view, had a 'magic wand' that gave to systems 'an appointed and harmonious order'. He showed history as the action of a single force, 'whose works are all wise and whose latest work is best'. He 'propitiated' science, religion and politics[2]. In short, he made everything palatable, reserving perhaps a special place for the violence and conflict which stuck so much in Acton's throat.

If Hegel had a 'magic wand', was the great 'propitiator', then Acton, and with him Schopenhauer, was pre-eminent amongst those who emphasised a static view of the world. The passage to which Acton refers when he repeats after Schopenhauer: 'history records that which is always the same' – merits in this context a substantial extract: 'The true philosophy of history', wrote Schopenhauer, 'always considers only what is unchanging and immutable, which is the same today as yesterday and always; it should therefore recognise what is identical in all the ancient and modern times, of the Orient and the Occident, and perceive the same humanity in spite of every difference in special circumstances, of costumes and customs. This, identical and enduring beneath all change, consists in the basic attributes of the human heart and head – many bad, few good. History should bear as its motto: the same, always different. If a man has read Herodotus, then, from a philosophic standpoint, he has studied enough history. For there there is everything that constitutes the subsequent history of the world: the activity, efforts, suffering and lot of humanity, as emerging from the above-named attributes, and the physical fate of the world'[3].

Such was the external pattern in which Acton saw embodied his own view of the contemporaneity of history. He might well have said with Schopenhauer that no historian could add anything to the writings of Herodotus. Such changes as had happened related only to the superficial and unimportant context of human life. They could not be taken to denote any change in the fundamental aspect of the treatment of man by man. 'Everything new is old', concludes Acton, 'especially in politics'[4].

Yet for all that, there still remains a difference in the meaning attributed to the pattern by the two thinkers. This had its origin in their widely differing systems. Schopenhauer's was determinist, atheist and metaphysically pessimistic. Acton believed in free will, God and in a metaphysical optimism. The system of morality derived from these basic tenets was the source of his distinction from Schopenhauer. History for Acton was anything but an illusion, even though he might qualify as illusory the subject-matter of most histories and historians.

What, then, did the pattern of contemporaneity mean to Acton? Amongst the notes there is a dictum taken from the French mystic Saint-Martin: '*Tout est contemporain pour celui qui connaît la notion de l'éternité*'[5]. Acton knew the notion of eternity; he gave to it the name of morality. It was this notion, entirely absent from Schopenhauer's thought, that gave meaning to the pattern, *i.e.* saw it not in its own light but in relation to a certain scale of values. If 'the main rules of morality' are applied all round, wrote Acton, history is converted 'into a frightful monument of sin'[6]; a monument compounded of man's inhumanity to man. This was the eternally contemporary in the flux of events, the unchanging theme disguised in an infinity of surface changes. But this, it is to be noted, is not a mystical, *a priori* judgment. Morality is neutral in its procedure. It only determines what is sought, not what is found. It is akin to a measuring-rod that does not of itself decide the length of what is to be measured. That length exists in its own right. All that morality does is to establish a criterion for the determination of the object, not in itself, but in relation to the ideal. It is this operation, and not a preconceived verdict that discloses 'a frightful monument of sin'.

In this way, despite all the changes in attendant circumstances, Acton could and did speak of 'a new Martyrology'. He did not distinguish between 'conquest, war in masses, negro slavery, manufacturers, oppression of the poor by the rich, ferocities of the criminal law'[7]. All these manifestations of the abuse of man by man stood on the same level when considered from the moral point of view, even though they might differ in every other respect, as indeed they did. The point is made correspondingly more specific in a note giving historical instances of the 'Martyrology'. Acton had a long memory. He could speak in the same breath of a massacre of four thousand Jews at Seville in 1391; of 'the French peasantry, from 1709; English factories described by Engels; Irish peasantry in 1846; India during the famines; the poverty of London; the Massacres of 1792, 1793; the retreat from Russia; American slavery; the Commune. What progress has come to, has not prevented all this, in the greater governments'[8]. On another occasion a note spoke of 'crime' as the enemy of progress: a crime manifested in persecution, torture, slavery, the Negro code, 'the jurists and judges who tormented and burnt witches, the authors of the machinery for sending souls to hell, at Ratisbon and Nuremberg. Not only the shippers and slave-drivers, but the lawgivers, the judges, the clergy were involved in this guilt. And this, not in the obscurity of the tenth century, on the verge of paganism and barbarism, but in the negotiations of Utrecht, etc'[9].

There is an important consequence of this analysis that itself illustrates how far-reaching was Acton's identification of the human passions involved. It concerns the problem of war, which for Acton, in contradistinction to most thinkers, could not be abstracted from the general picture of inhumanity. It was merely another aspect of the same phenomenon. There were, he wrote, 'cognate states of mind' involved in wars, religious persecution, trials for witchcraft and the cruelties practised on criminals[10].

All that has been said so far might be grouped under the general and abstract heading of contemporary historical *situations*. These, however, were nothing but the work of men, who themselves therefore could not escape the stigma originating in their association with the situation. Consequently, turning from the abstract to the particular, Acton's view committed him to a recognition of the existence of individual criminals striding through history. Once again, how could there be a crime if there were no criminals to be held responsible for its perpetration? Acton explicity held this view. Murder, he taught his Cambridge listeners, was 'not an epidemic peculiar to any time, or any country, or any opinion'. It was 'one characteristic of modern monarchy', he added. Amongst history's 'anointed culprits' he instanced Elizabeth Tudor (who ordered the execution of Mary Stuart), William III (who ordered the Massacre at Glencoe); and Napoleon (who ordered the liquidation of the Duc d'Enghien)[11]. Acton saw no reason to exempt any of these from the same judgment he would have passed on a murderer who acted for private motives and not for *raison d'état*. It was these and their like who, corrupted by the power at their disposal, were an indispensable factor in making of history what Acton once called 'an awful agony'[12]. Even more bitter, perhaps, was his condemnation of the historians who had 'praise and hero-worship' for the 'anointed culprits'. 'The strong man with the dagger is followed by the weaker man with the sponge. First, the criminal who slays; then the sophist who defends the slayer'[13].

The contemporaneity of history may also now be considered from a second aspect. The abuse of man shows only one side of the picture. The other side, distinct, however inseparably connected, displays the complementary public elements. The abuse could only be possible if certain conditions were observed – conditions relating to the conduct of public life.

For Acton there existed only two kinds of politics – Machiavellian and moral. The first was characterised by a lack of respect for man, whereas the second made this respect its foremost, perhaps even its only principle. This was the overriding, qualitative distinction. It offered the means of separating the sheep from the goats. But it did not mean of course that there might not be any number of different coloured goats. Although moral politics might be considered *en bloc*, immoral Machiavellian politics might show very important quantitative distinctions, whilst still remaining within the same immoral category. It has already been seen, for example, how party politics, with all their deficiencies, could yet be the 'most moral of all'[14].

Given the *ultimate* distinction however, Acton considered all past and present politics to be characterised in a varying degree by Machiavellianism. How could it be otherwise for one who knew 'the notion of eternity', *i.e.* for one who had the conception of moral politics? In Acton's writings Machiavelli, and such of his disciples as Talleyrand occupy a position quite disproportionate to that allotted them elsewhere. Where they are treated as phenomena of a limited importance in time and place, Acton attributed to them an importance transcending these limitations. Indeed, Acton was probably fascinated by Machiavelli. He could respect him for his honesty in being dishonest. He, at least, was not among the weak men 'with a sponge' who followed the strong man 'with a dagger'. Machiavelli had the courage of his lack of conviction. He felt no need to whitewash Caesar Borgia. Acton admired and was fascinated.

This was the basis of his treatment of Talleyrand's *Memoirs*. He detested their author of course – as 'the unscrupulous priest, the money-getting Sybarite, the patient auxiliary of the conqueror and the tyrant, the Royalist who defended the tenth of August, the Republican minister who brought on the Empire, the imperial dignitary who brought on the Bourbons, the apostle of legitimacy who hailed its fall'. Such was the indictment of suppleness and accommodation. Yet when Acton also wrote that 'Talleyrand . . . was not good on a sinking ship' the expression reveals more than a sneaking admiration. Furthermore, when Acton draws from the *Memoirs* the lesson that 'it is the note of a strong man to employ principles and of a weak man to obey them', the inference has a universal application. Again, Acton's regret that Talleyrand was 'too well bred', too much the *grand seigneur* to describe his successes, or to reveal, for example, 'the arts of management by which a senate peopled with regicides was brought to declare for the Bourbons', the regret derives from the gap thereby occasioned in the completeness of the symbolic politician[15].

But Talleyrand was only Machiavelli's pupil. What of the master? There is, to begin with, a striking parallel in the circumstances of Machiavelli's withdrawal and return, and that of Acton. It was after the former's loss of the Florentine

Secretaryship of State, and his imprisonment, torture and exile that he began to compose *The Prince*. It was then that Machiavelli, removed from the seat of power, turned in his hut to what he called the 'true nourishment' of the mind. Acton's eclipse was by no means so spectacular. To a superficial eye, indeed, it might seem that the peer, the courtier, the confidant of Gladstone and the habitué of political clubs stood closer to affairs of state than the thirty-year-old Member of Parliament. Yet this ignores the realities of the situation. No less than Machiavelli did Acton clash with authority and in the contest lose the title to a power that he warmly cherished. (It is irrelevant to point out that the intellectual dominion claimed by Acton differed by far from Machiavelli's political aspirations. It is the impulse that counts.) No less than Machiavelli was Acton reduced to sitting on the sidelines, condemned to observe a game he was forbidden to play. Acton's Aldenham library may well be compared to Machiavelli's rustic hut. There sat in both, brooding in disenchantment on the past, the present and future, two thwarted men of action.

But if Acton's diagnosis of politics as a struggle for power coincided with Machiavelli's, this does not at all mean that his remedy was identical. Acton was as eclectic here as elsewhere. He utterly rejected the notion that politics or public life actually be based on coming to terms with an urge responsible for so much misery. There was another way. The abuse of power was not an unalterable fact of nature.

As a specific historical phenomenon, Acton took the conventional view of Machiavelli as the theorist of the modern nation state, released from the nominal supremacy of the medieval Papacy. The state now became a law unto itself. Acton summed up the theory in these terms: 'The first paramount fact with which modern history begins is that the state is above right and wrong. While it pursues its own objects, acquires power, increases territory, promotes prosperity, raises the renown or gratifies the pride of the nation, it is not to be prevented or censured because it employs the basest of crimes, the taking of human life by war, or by the tribunal, or by the assassin . . . if the man (*i.e.* the national hero) is great, do not grudge him the stepping-stones of his greatness'[16].

This was Machiavelli's historical location. It gave the circumstances in which the theory of *The Prince* had its origin and which inevitably conditioned the theory itself. But this background, or soil, as in Acton's analogous approach to the Romantic movement, was by far the least important of Machiavelli's attributes. The real question was to determine the truth or falsity of the theory. In this respect Acton was in no doubt. The Florentine was supremely significant as the analyst *par excellence* of politics. Acton found him 'an excellent man unjustly maligned'[17]. The injustice was all the more reprehensible, for Machiavelli's 'political veracity' had been tested and proved by the three centuries following his death, *i.e.* the seventeenth, eighteenth and nineteenth centuries[18]. 'Few can throw a stone at him', noted Acton, 'not the admirers of Elizabeth, Mary, Cromwell, James II, William III, Napoleon, neither Orangeman nor Jacobite, nor Bonapartist'. Immediately following this note, he quotes an unnamed author's *Vindication of Machiavel:* 'Who intends to express a dishonest man calls him a Machiavellian; they might as well say, he was a Straffordian, or a Malborian'[19]. If Strafford, or Marlborough, or James II, why not a host of others? In the Introduction that he contributed to L. A. Burd's edition of *The Prince*, Acton displayed part of his vast and sometimes curious scholarship in tracing the Machiavellian affiliation of many of these others. He drew examples from virtually the whole of Europe, from the sixteenth to the nineteenth century, from thinkers, statesmen, politicians. The Introduction was a brilliant essay in the mode of relating a multitude of different circumstances to the operation of a single principle. In a necessarily brief selection, Acton spoke of Catherine de Medici, Francis Bacon, Cromwell, Cardinals Retz and Richelieu, Morley, Carlyle, Hegel, Mommsen and Fichte as all adherents of one or more of the elements of the doctrine. For Hegel the course of world history stood beyond virtue, vice or justice; Fichte thought it absurd to robe a prince in the cowl of a monk; Carlyle held that might was right; Ranke that the best touchstone was time; Morley maintained that men of action must be judged by the standards of men of action; and Napoleon's maxim was to judge a man solely by the results that he achieved. 'The authentic interpreter of Machiavelli . . .' concluded Acton, 'is the whole of later history'[20]. In a lecture he said that Machiavelli 'reduced to a code the wickedness of public men'[21]. He could cite abundant evidence.

This catalogue of Machiavellians, illustrious and extensive though it is, still does not exhaust his significance. To treat him as purely and simply the guide to three centuries would indeed be an untenable *locus standi.* It would not be enough merely to say that the theory and practice of Machiavelli's time 'resembles nothing so much as the theory and practice of ours'[22]. If, as Acton repeatedly wrote, 'passions and needs do not change', then how could it be reasonable to suppose that what applied to the seventeenth, eighteenth and nineteenth centuries should not also apply to earlier centuries? Acton made in fact no such limitation. He held the Machiavellian diagnosis to be of well-nigh timeless significance.

In writing that 'the monument' to the memory of Caesar Borgia (*i.e. The Prince*) 'has secretly fascinated half the politicians in the world'[23], Acton was making on his own confession a parlous underestimate; he was omitting the other half from the operation of a universal judgment. Acton's appreciation of Machiavelli reaches its purest, simplest and culminating point when he notes that he 'really defines the separation of ethics and politics – common practice reduced to theory'[24].

This separation was the precondition to the abuse of man. Both phenomena were interdependent and both expressed different aspects of the same reality. Acton's analysis included in its scope the whole range of socio-political activity. He saw a certain solidarity and interdependence of evil which, if it appeared in public life, would infallibly extend to and determine the abuse of man. Conversely, if man were abused, the eye was inevitably turned to the existence of the abuse of politics. Acton saw the same cause and effect working their way through every facet of the individual and collective existence of man. All would partake in some degree at least, of the omnipresence of an immorality that had but to show itself in one field for its effects to spread to every other. The same reality manifested itself, for example, in the slave trade and in official corruption – and this had necessarily to be the case, for the two were interdependent. Once again, it was all or nothing.

This picture may be summed up in another way. The contemporaneity of history in its reference to the actual condition of man can also be characterised as a constant tension and crisis, arising from the contrast between what ought to be and what is. The perennial crisis, to which Acton's analysis points, differs from a critical set of circumstances in that it identifies not a localised or ephemeral situation but one that broods constantly over the human situation *as such*, penetrating deep into every aspect of human existence. Man is born to be respected; but he is at all times abused. In this contrast is born the crisis, the perennial crisis of man.

> *Between the Idea*
> *And the Reality*
> *Between the Motion –*
> *And the Act*
> *Falls the shadow*[25].

This view affiliates Acton to the great pessimists of thought. If the underlying truth of history is its contemporaneity, then every human endeavour is marked with futility; every ideology appears but a new excuse for mutual conflict; every religion but a cloak for persecution; every discovery but a new form of enslavement. Acton's voice is that of Ecclesiastes: 'There is nothing new under the sun'. It is the voice of Schopenhauer. It is, with some reservation, also the voice of Burckhardt, who saw history's 'constant' in 'suffering, striving and acting man, as he is, always was, and will be'[26]. Again, it is the voice of thinkers, such as Spengler and Nietzsche, who saw man bound to an eternal cycle of repetition. If Acton is placed amongst his contemporaries, then in this respect he belongs amongst the anti-Hegelian nineteenth-century pessimists.

Yet Acton, like any Hegelian, also believed in progress. The notion of the contemporaneity of history did not exhaust the potentiality of the world. Man could escape from his plight; the perennial crisis could be resolved; the theme of history could be transformed. To the truth embodied in the contemporaneity of history there was again a 'balancing truth' – the possibility of progress. What did Acton understand by progress and how was it to be achieved?

CHAPTER V

Progress in History

NIETZSCHE once asked the question: 'Who can bear the idea of Eternal Recurrence?' In an epigram he formulated the thought at its most extreme: 'Let us consider this idea in its most terrifying form: existence, as it is, without meaning or goal, but inescapably recurrent, without a finale into nothingness....' What Acton understood by the contemporaneity of history bears sufficient resemblance to the Nietzschean view for the same question to emerge. Could the notion be borne that human destiny offered no release from the perennial crisis encompassing human life? Could the notion be borne that the future of man should be as overcast as his past and present?

Those whose analysis brought them to this point tended either to take refuge in some form of aesthetic contemplation as, for example, Schopenhauer and Burckhardt or actually to welcome the prospect of a hopeless future. 'Optimism is cowardice', wrote Spengler. In either case a certain abdication of will and self-confidence was involved. Those whose reaction took the form of aesthetic contemplation justified Acton's occasional warnings about the danger of art. It was not for nothing that he warned the reader of his Hundred Best Books 'to steel' himself against literary beauties and charms[1]. They constituted not only a refuge from reality but also a positive distraction from the task of grappling with reality.

Acton's reaction to the human position disclosed by history varied radically from that of his apparent fellow-pessimists. Acton indeed, if Nietzche's question be put to him, could obviously not bear the vision. But his argument against the pessimists and their like is anything but personal. The fact is that Acton believed in a certain kind of progress. How was this at all possible? How could a man to whom history revealed so many 'false dawns' – to borrow a phrase from Aldous Huxley – so many broken hopes and unfulfilled promises, so many rulers 'who began well only to end ill', not take refuge either in cynicism or in some kind of withdrawal? Acton saw the world much as did Horatio. He too could speak,

> *Of carnal, bloody and unnatural acts;*
> *Of accidental judgments, casual slaughters;*
> *Of deaths put on by cunning, and forc'd cause,*
> *And, in this upshot, purposes mistook*
> *Fall'n on the inventors' heads.*

Yet despite this, Acton's conviction of progress, remained unaffected.

It was the notion of morality that supplied his *point de départ*. If man was born to be respected, was entitled to be respected, then it could not but be rational to suppose that this respect would at one time come to characterise his existence. In other words – and this is characteristic of Acton's dialectic method of thought – it is precisely the notion of the contemporaneity of history that inspires and provokes the notion of progress. It is precisely *because* history shows so little variation in man's status that this status must be transformed. It would not be reasonable, Acton is saying, were the history of humanity to be confined to a sorry tale of oppression. More than that, he continues, it would be a denial of the divine image reflected in man that he should *eternally* be fated to be exploited or enslaved or persecuted or terrorised. History, he writes, 'is a scene of guilt, a record of sin and crime. The wicked flourish like the bay-tree. The virtuous expect to suffer persecution. . . . That gives an imperfect vision of Providence, of divine wisdom and omnipotence – unless you can show progress. Divine judgements won't do'[2]. Thus – 'not to believe in progress is to question the divine government', or without progress 'there is no *raison d'être* for the world'[3].

That Acton held this view with almost literal insistence is evident from his critical attitude to Newman. In a letter to Gladstone he described Newman as 'by far the best writer the Church of Rome has had in England since the Reformation'. Yet the same letter continues: 'if Newman's writings and religion are "worked out" it is a school of Infidelity'[4]. Why was Newman an Infidel? An explanation, even if only partial, is to be found in a note. It refers to Newman's denial of progress. 'History mocked and depressed him', wrote Acton. 'He discerned no progress . . . Note that Newman denies the divine government of the world. Providence does not manifest itself in history. The law of progress is not the law of history'[5].

What did Acton understand by 'the law of progress' that would give the world its *raison d'être?* Before answering, and as a preliminary to answering, it is first of all necessary to examine what the law did not mean. This was the view of progress that, frequently associated with anti-Catholicism, had its origin in the eighteenth century and reached its apogee in the early twentieth century. At the base of the doctrine lay the achievements of natural science in apparently subjecting to human control larger and larger spheres of man's environment. History was taken to be an advance towards more such achievements with their concomitant result in the increase of man's happiness and freedom. Acton's frequent appreciative references to Voltaire and Gibbon show that he was by no means unsympathetic to certain aspects of the eighteenth-century movement, and especially to its anti-Catholicism[6]. Furthermore, Acton also partially identified himself with a series of affiliated thinkers when he jocularly called the 'Fathers' of the 'liberal Church'. He mentioned Leslie Stephen, Pierre Bayle, Turgot, Washington, Jefferson, Bentham, Benjamin Constant, Tocqueville, Macaulay and Mill[7]. But the identification was only partial. It referred only to certain demands made by both the liberals and Acton, such as toleration, universal education and freedom of the press. Far more important was the substance of the difference between them. This Acton summed up by saying that their progress was 'the religion of those that have none'[8].

His own, on the other hand, was that of a man who defiantly had a religion, even though it might not seem to fit into any orthodox category. The idea in itself of progress, could logically be deduced *a priori* from this religion. It also 'balanced' – in Acton's term – the notion of the contemporaneity of history. Of what precisely did it consist? What was the progress that fulfilled the essential role in Acton's religious sphere? There was, firstly, progress in knowledge and ideas. The corollary to the statement in the Inaugural Lecture that 'the earthly wants and passions of men remain almost unchanged' is 'an advance of knowledge' and 'a development of ideas'. In this context, and then as examples of method, Acton mentioned only scientists – Darwin, Sir Robert Ball, Faraday and John Hunter amongst others[9]. In many of the notes this limitation is broken down. The claim is even made that as nothing else changes, 'the true subject of history' and the only thing worth studying is knowledge and thought[10]. There were also occasions when Acton said of himself that he rejected the study of 'laws' and 'institutions' in favour of the study of ideas – for 'the progress is in ideas'[11].

This was of course an exaggerated and inconsistent conclusion. But it does illustrate the importance of ideas in the pattern of progress. Even so, on their own, they were clearly insufficient to remove history from its status as 'a scene of guilt, a record of sin and crime'. Ideas on their own would still 'give an imperfect vision of providence'. On the contrary, since Acton's criticism of history can be reduced to the contrast between actuality and the ideas proclaimed, it might even seem that the progress of ideas and thought would accentuate and intensify the contrast.

No, what was required, were Providence to be fulfilled, was nothing less than the collective release of men from their 'human bondage'. Acton cherished the messianic hope, couched in this-worldly terms of respect for the human personality. It was because he saw, despite every discouragement, the possibility – or rather the certainty – of this millenium that in the ultimate resort, *he* was not mocked or depressed by history. This redemption, in the form of the embodiment of perfect morality, was logically necessary in order fully to compensate for the trials of the imperfect morality of history. In the ultimate resort Acton's attitude towards the world was positive. That is to say, an approximate distinction must be drawn separating the negative view of the world as irremediably imperfect, and hence as the preliminary to a future world that would right the wrongs of the present, and the positive view of the world as containing within itself the potentiality of millenial transformation.

If Acton be not reckoned an adherent of the latter view, then his historical philosophy makes no sense at all.

Entirely apart from the question of morality with its insistence on the respect due to man, Acton's tone when speaking of the world is that of an outraged idealist cherishing a certain vision. He is outraged at the spectacle he must witness, whether in the past or present. The implication in every case is inescapable and unmistakable. When Acton protests at slavery, the protest is simultaneously a demand for liberty. The same applies of course to all his many other attacks on selected aspects of reality. The demand is contained in the attack, to such an extent that were the moral ideal never made explicit, it would none the less emerge crystal-clear of its own accord.

The presuppositions that emerge in this manner supply the framework of progress. This can also be approached through the medium of the explicitly formulated demands. Thus Acton held 'the object of civil Society' to be 'Justice – not truth, Virtue, Wealth, Knowledge, Glory, Power. Justice is followed by Equality and Liberty'[12]. 'What we uphold', he writes elsewhere, '[is] Charity, Toleration, relief of poverty, Scientific Enlightenment and Progress, public faith, absence of the lust for power, peace and economy, spotless justice, no oppression, purity of public men. But what we most want is liberty of conscience'[13]. If the transition is made from these abstract outlines to concrete terms, then Acton is found describing progress as 'consideration for the individual, not for society; wounded and captive, accused prisoner; condemned convict; afflicted in body or in mind; indigent poor; the very old and very young; the sick man and the exposed'[14].

In drawing up this framework Acton was apparently merely drawing further into the future certain demands and phenomena that had already made their historical appearance. Yet progress required more than the realisation of the demands and the perfection of the phenomena, in that it also required their separation from the imperfections that deformed them at the level of history. Acton once accused himself saying 'things that were at first sight grossly inconsistent, without attempting to reconcile them'[15]. Nowhere perhaps does this apply more than in the case of the theory of progress.

The theory seems to amount to a series of inconsistencies. To all appearances, the various factors associated with progress contradict each other. For example, could anything for Acton be more grossly contradictory than to see no incompatibility between equality and liberty? Surely the two are mutually exclusive? Numerous other examples are worthy of mention in their turn.

Acton wrote – jocularly perhaps – that *Fabrikgesetzgebung* (factory legislation) was 'a sign of progress'[16]. Yet he also feared the day when 'Parliament will do more and more'. Elsewhere he wrote: 'Property, not conscience, is the basis of liberty'[17]. Yet he contradicts this by also asserting that 'liberty is the reign of conscience'[18]. Should it not be the reign of property? Both apparently cannot be true. Again, Acton opposed popular election as a system of government, for 'from the absolute will of an entire people – there is no appeal, no redemption, no refuge but treason'[19]. Yet he also wrote that popular election 'would ensure integrity and capacity in the rulers'. The whole nation would 'have a share in controlling the government under which it lives'[20]. There is, finally, the matter of power where the most striking contradiction seems to prevail. If power corrupts, how can public men be pure? How can 'spotless justice' be attainable? Acton, as he said himself, did not attempt to reconcile his inconsistencies. Yet for the student they are too numerous and pervasive to be left unexplained. How may an explanation be sought?

The answer lies in the fact of the world's existence at two levels – there is the real that is reality and the ideal that is not yet reality. As a result of this co-existence penetration by the ideal into the real is accompanied by distortion, deformation and confusion. The good is confounded with the bad. Excellent impulses and ideas that belong to the ideal as necessary constituents may not only lose their ideal character but also turn into pillars of the real. The notion of progress, on the other hand, demands that the ideal be retained in its purity. Thus the same idea can exist in both an ideal and a real form. If the inconsistencies mentioned above are examined in this light, then it becomes possible to reconcile them. Equality and liberty, for example, are as ideas not necessarily incompatible. It is when they are pursued by political means in the real world that they succumb to incompatibility. A similar contradiction prevails in the case of factory legislation. It is rightly identified as a sign of progress, for it incorporates partially at least, the principle of charity. On the other hand, the manner of its operation involves the extension of centralised power with all the nefarious possibilities arising from this. Progress consists in the attaining of the one without the other. When Acton discusses in contradictory terms the basis of liberty, the same principle is involved. If the basis of liberty is property, then this is, rightly or wrongly an analysis that refers to the world of Acton's day. The propertyless, the worker, is at a hopeless disadvantage when engaged in a duel with the propertied, *i.e.* the man who 'supplies seconds, arms and ammunition'. He is deprived of his liberty as a consequence. He has no property to back up his claim, and must perforce yield to the man who has. But the fact of this being so is a condemnation of the world that permits such conditional liberty, rather than a denial of the possible universal and unconditional union of liberty and conscience. Finally, again, there is the question of power. In the real world the characteristic of power is its association with corruption of one kind or another. But – and this fact in itself signifies both the nearness and the distance of the real and the ideal – Acton nowhere suggests that power as a social factor is incompatible with progress. He does not say with Burckhardt for example that 'Power is of its nature evil, whoever wields it. It is not a stability but a lust, and *eo ipso* insatiable, therefore unhappy in itself and doomed to make others unhappy'[21]. On the contrary, not only does Acton not say this, but despite all the evidence of history to the contrary he was able to envisage power in another context altogether. Not only could he demand 'purity in public men' but he could also write: 'authority that does not exist for liberty is not authority, but force. It has no sanction'[22].

This may all be summed up in Acton's definition of progress as 'the superiority of ethical motives over physical, of man over nature' or as the 'increase of mental over material objects'[23]. If ethical motives prevail over physical, then liberty depends not on property but on conscience, power does not entail corruption, and equality does not exclude liberty. In each case the physical or material factors deforming the ideal, with all their nefarious ramifications and consequences, yield to a purification of that which already exists.

Acton does not go beyond these general characteristics of the ideal. He does not discuss progress in detail. He was doubtless more concerned with bringing progress about than with describing what lay at the end of the journey. The means to the end were of more importance than the end itself. It lay nearer his heart to attack the existing order than to delineate its replacement. The task was so urgent, the tension so great, that constructive consideration of the future had to yield to the need of destroying what stood in the way of the future.

What was this obstacle? The enemy was the past and present, *i.e.* history. It was this that stood in the way of the future, for if all history is contemporary then past and present are one, and only the future can conceivably enjoy the possibility of escape and redemption. It follows from this that progress cannot be susceptible of gradual attainment. Any transitional period that might otherwise be considered would inevitably succumb to history's capacity for confounding the good with the evil. Progress would be removed farther and farther into the future. Any interval between history and the realisation of progress would thus be indefinitely – even infinitely – prolonged. In effect, gradual progress, in Acton's use of the word, is a contradiction in terms. Progress must therefore take on the form of a sudden transformation, an apocalyptic change, a sharp cutting adrift from history. This is what Acton had in mind when he spoke of the Revolution. 'What was the Revolution?' he asked himself, and he answered: 'The defeat of History. History dethroned'[24].

It is in respect of *this* revolution that Acton can be said to be a revolutionary or a radical. Once again, as in the case of *Romantik*, liberal, progress, a familiar term is used with a distinctive and specialised meaning. He himself defines the two meanings that he gave to the terms: 'Radicalism is the ignoring, the negation of History. But that is appeasable and superficial, compared with the Radicalism that is extracted from the knowledge of history – that the awful agony should come to an end – ages that believed in astrology and witchcraft, torture and arbitrary prison, plague-stricken prisons, exquisite misery of death, slave trade, penal laws, the worst crimes committed by law, no protection against crime, or against disease or pain'[25].

Acton's treatment of the French Revolution can be used as an illustration of his thesis. Not only was it the most 'revolutionary' event in his immediate historical perspective but also, and perhaps for this very reason, he devoted to it much of his attention, including a series of lectures. As a result, the distinction between the two types of Radicalism can be effectively traced on the actual historical plane and not merely on the theoretical.

Acton once defined 'the essence' of liberalism as 'not to believe in the sanctity of the past'[26]. In this sense the revolutionaries were certainly liberal and Acton in principle could welcome their efforts. He could share to the full in their belief that the old régime must be destroyed and a just order inaugurated in its stead. Did the Revolution achieve this? The answer is best given in the words with which Acton heralded the Fourth of August, 'the most decisive date in the Revolution', he said[27]. All the events, up to the emergence of Bonaparte in 1799 he fitted into the following framework: 'The Revolution will never be intelligibly known to us until we discover its conformity to the common law, and recognise that it is not utterly singular and exceptional, that other scenes have been as horrible as these, and many men as bad'[28]. This does not of course mean that Acton's treatment forbore from discussing the various phases of the Revolution, the different type of personalities and social forces involved, the different political theories that were thrown up, or the impact of events outside France. But it does mean that the intention was to relate the narration to the moral view. Such incidents central to the Revolution, and by no means on its periphery, as for the example, the September Massacres or the Reign of Terror, could not but be expressive of the 'common law'. Acton quotes with derision Jefferson's justification of the September Massacres: 'Many guilty persons fell without the forms of trial, and with them some innocent. These I deplore as much as anybody. But – it was necessary to use the arm of the people, a machine not quite so blind as balls and bombs, but blind to a certain degree – was ever such a prize won with so little innocent blood?'[29]. If this condemnation was justified, then Acton was obliged to see in the practice of the Revolution, as distinct from its theoretical claims, a very large degree of involvement in the past that it had allegedly set out to destroy. His appreciation of the principle at stake did not blind him to the distance separating its realisation from the ideal configuration. The French Revolution, in fact, was nothing more than a parody of the true revolution.

This conclusion can be reached in another way – by considering the effects of the Revolution. As a young man Acton had quoted approvingly Tocqueville's thesis enunciated in *L'Ancien Régime et la Révolution*. He rendered it as follows: 'That the French Revolution, far from reversing the political spirit of the old State, only carried out the same principle with intenser energy. The State, which was absolute before, became still more absolute, and the organs of the popular will become more efficient agents for the exercise of arbitrary power'[30]. The mature Acton, writing some thirty years later, was able to trace the further impact of this initial involvement. He noted for example: 'The revolutionary theory made homogeneous nations. Equal and alike. No class interests. This leads (1) to nationality – for sake of homogeneousness; (2) to socialism for the destruction of classes'; and again: 'Military organisation begins with the French Revolution. But remember Charles VII. It is the product of a Republic – of nationality, democracy and patriotism, imitated by Germany and Russia'[31]. If these deductions were valid, then a radicalism of this nature, its nefarious roots in the past putting forth nefarious branches into the present, was indeed 'appeasable, superficial'. It was indeed the mere negation and not the dethronement of history.

Acton's sympathy for the principle of revolution in the abstract made it by no means easy for him to acknowledge this distinction. In fact, in his anxiety to defend the Revolution against romantic detractors who saw in it a breach with the past, Acton actually fell into the paradoxical trap of claiming for it a historical ancestry. In his defence he wrote that it was 'itself historic' and had 'roots that could be profitably traced far back in the ages'[32]. Elsewhere he spoke of it as a breach 'with the immediate past . . . but a return to the remoter Past, to ideas which were rooted in the depths of history'[33]. Proceeding further on these lines he was even able to speak with approval and sympathy of 'the revolutionary historians who argue with some show of reason that the atrocities were not due to the spirit abroad at the time, but to that which had been nurtured in France for ages before'[34].

This may well be true, but in Acton's mouth it is astounding reasoning. It testifies to the power of the emotional factor involved in his desire to have done with history. But he did not of course succumb. When it came to the point, he disregarded the special pleading that would exclude the revolutionary, but include the inquisitor. An unfinished note, all the more eloquent for breaking off in the middle of a sentence is sufficiently explicit: 'Louis Blanc means that the apologists of St Bartholomew have no right to complain, are mere hypocrites if they complain of Danton and Marat. He forgets that this can be reversed, that the apologists of

September"[35]. If the *ancien régime* had its St Bartholomew, had not the new its September Massacres? Both might be cogently defended but the basis in *raison d'état* would in each case be the same. The justification in each case would therefore necessarily appear to Acton as an unconvincing superstructure designed to conceal the reality of human conflict. Again the radicalism had shown itself to be 'appeasable, superficial'. What, then, was true radicalism?

CHAPTER VI

The Task of History

IN the last resort Acton was obliged to condemn the French Revolution on account of the identity of its methods with those of the *ancient régime*. It constituted in no way a breach with the past but only provided a different set of aims, policies and theories with which to justify the self-same treatment of man by man. The superstructure might be different but the substructure was unchanged. The French Revolution represented an attempt at overcoming an imperfect history by using the very methods characteristic of imperfection. It had thereby condemned itself to failure. This was emphatically not the sort of revolution that Acton had in mind.

In a larger context than the political, had he thereby debarred himself from acting on the world? This conclusion would be entirely unwarranted. Apart from the fact that to deny the possibility of effective action would have contradicted Acton's positive attitude *vis-à-vis* the world, an attitude of resignation or withdrawal would have been tantamount to acquiescence in the *status quo*. To say, as Acton did, that 'political indifference signifies moral indifference' is sufficiently explicit[1]. But these were the two antithetical poles of politics: a self-defeating activity, however high-minded and well-meaning its protagonists, and a passivity, leaving the world to stew in its own juice. In the end the former achieved the same lack of result as the latter.

The revolution that Acton urged was intellectual in origin. He was an idealist in the sense that he believed in the power of the ideal to shape the real in the image of the ideal. If Acton believed in the inevitability of the millenium, then this was only conditional on the co-operation of human effort. It would not be attained of its own accord – even though it had to be attained. The actual agency of such human effort was history itself, with the historian its prime agent. At this point the final dialectic element in Acton's scheme manifests itself, for he would use history, as the incorporation of the ideal, to destroy the real. From this confrontation of opposites he foresaw the synthesis of both – the realised ideal. History would teach the method of overthrowing its own mastery. It would be in truth an archimedean lever wherewith to overturn the world. This constituted Acton's panoramic vision of the culminating point of history and human destiny. His tone is rarely rhetorical or emotional. His version of the prophetic anticipation of the day when the lion will lie down with the lamb and the swords be beaten into ploughshares is couched in rather *terre à terre* terms. Yet the identity of vision is unmistakable: 'if Pagan and Christian can honestly find room to differ about Julian, French and English about Napoleon, Loyalist and Republican about Washington, Protestant and Catholic about Luther, Whig and Tory about Burke – History teaches in vain'[2]. It was because history had this exalted function to fulfil that Acton condemned so harshly and unforgivingly those historians who had, in his eyes, betrayed their trust. Nothing less than the destiny of man was at stake.

What was required of history in order that it might achieve

its aim of reconciling man and man in accordance with the Messianic hope? How was history to ensure that it did not teach in vain? The operative word, here as elsewhere, is 'history'. Acton speaks not of historians in the plural but of history in the singular. The reason for this was obvious in so far that as an individual the historian must disappear. A 'history independent of historians' was one of Acton's hopes'[3]. The same point recurred in his circular to the contributors to the *Cambridge Modern History*. He had then expressed the hope that only the list of contributors would show 'where the Bishop of Oxford laid down the pen, and whether Fairbairn or Gasquet, Liebermann or Harrison took it up'[4]. Again, in his survey at Cambridge of various writings on the French Revolution, he could look forward to 'a golden age' when 'our history' would be 'certain'[5].

Probably no historian has ever existed who did not claim for his work the virtue of certainty. (Even those historians who disclaim its existence still claim the virtue.) What, therefore, does certainty mean as far as Acton is concerned? It may be roughly defined as the final stage reached when history has passed through the various phases described in earlier chapters. That is to say, if the historical viewpoint of the romantic is expressed without let or hindrance, to be then subsumed and overcome by that of the liberal, again without let or hindrance, then the result is an otherwise unattainable degree of certainty. Into neither phase, given the perfect conditions postulated by Acton, does there enter anything personal, anything that would betray the sympathy, position or circumstances of the historian. In the first phase he acts purely and simply as the mouthpiece of reality; in the second, purely and simply as the mouthpiece of morality. Given Acton's presuppositions, how could any scope for uncertainty thereby arise? In other words the final truth of history lay outside history. It was removed from the sphere of change and located in the sphere of timelessness. It did not belong to the historian, even though he it was who made truth articulate. It belonged rather to the world.

For the sake of an example, let the career of Napoleon be taken. This has been depicted from every conceivable angle. But this variety is by no means a disadvantage. An advocate, both prosecuting and defending, can still aid the judge. A party-writer, said Acton with characteristic humour, 'would not have done so well from the mere inspiration of disinterested veracity'[6]. The historian can by no means afford to neglect the party-writers. But just as little can he afford to adopt exclusively a similarly time-conditioned standpoint. He subsumes time in the eternal, *i.e.* he sees in one consolidated vision both the temporal and the eternal context and impact of Napoleon's career. With one and the same vision he sees his political conduct and his private life, his economic policy and his military strategy, his constitutional plans and his administrative reforms. The resulting depiction finally owes nothing to the historian but everything to the timeless vision of which he is the exponent. If Napoleon, to take a very simple aspect indeed of his career, ordered the liquidation of the Duc d'Enghien, then this was sufficient for him to stand condemned in Acton's eyes as a murderer. On the other hand, in another respect, Napoleon is also included, together with Augustus, Peter the Great, Mehemet Ali and others amongst 'the worst men [who] have sometimes made the best and ablest rulers'[7]. The vision in each case is universal and impartial. It is indisputable. History is removed from history.

This conception of impartiality as universality has little in common with what is customarily understood by the term. Acton made no such attempt to be fair, or to be neutral, as the term impartiality usually suggests. He was not concerned with letting the facts speak of their own accord, for the simple reason that facts of their own accord are unable to speak. His attitude may therefore usefully be contrasted with that of Ranke, a contrast often made by Acton himself. To begin with, Acton had abundant praise for Ranke's freedom from partiality. He had no axe to grind. He was free of national or religious bias[8]. From this negative point of view there are few historians for whom Acton seems to have had as much respect and admiration. True, Ranke is included amongst the Machiavellians for having written '*der beste Prüfstein ist die Zeit*'[9]. But he does not rank amongst the historians of 'demoralised sympathies', as do Carlyle and Macaulay, for example[10].

However, to be free from partiality is by no means synonymous with impartiality – in Acton's meaning. Ranke's sins were not those of commission but the far more subtle and therefore more dangerous sins of omission. He refused, it is true, to allow active prejudice to distort his narration, but the air of objectivity that he thereby achieved was spurious. The criticism that Acton had made in his youth of Mr Knight's *History of England* may well be referred to again. 'His fairness', he wrote of Knight, 'is the negative spirit of indifference, which treats all men alike with distant respect, not an intelligent justice, *suum cuique tribuens*'[11].

It is not difficult to see how this applies to Ranke. The difference separating him from Acton is summed up in an epigram: 'A convinced man differs from a prejudiced man as an honest man differs from a liar'[12], *i.e.* conviction is not equated with prejudice. If Ranke, therefore, did not share the same conviction as Acton, he was unable to detect the same 'reality', for this 'reality' had no meaning in its own right but depended for this on what the historian made of it.

If he himself had no conviction, as Acton alleged of Ranke, then he had no recourse but to succumb to the fallacy of seeing that 'reality' in its own light – '*Wie es eigentlich gewesen ist*', as Ranke said of himself. But no facts ever speak for themselves. If this is apparently the case, what has really happened is that 'reality' has become its own criterion – the arch-sin. The historian has limited himself to a purely romantic view of his subject, with all that is thereby implied. What Ranke really did, according to Acton, was derive his attitude from time and place. His attitude was the very reverse of impartial and universal; it was localised and subjective.

Ranke, said Acton, 'spoke of transactions and occurrences when it would be safe to speak of turpitude and crime'[13]. He referred at least twice to one such 'transaction' or 'crime' – depending on the point of view – as though it had made some deep impression on him: it was the massacre at Glencoe in 1682. He mentioned it in the Inaugural Lecture and again in the *Lectures on Modern History*. If William III was responsible for ordering the massacre of this Catholic clan, as Acton believed, then this afforded 'a basis for judging the character of William and his government'[14]. In other words, the king and his government were no better than murderers. Acton pointed out, however, that this was not the conclusion drawn by Ranke. He did not, of course, conceal the fact that William ordered the massacre. But he failed to draw from this action the inevitable conclusion. Acton complained that when Ranke came to sum up William's life, 'Glencoe is forgotten, the imputation of murder drops, like a thing unworthy of notice'[15]. In his notes he commented that Ranke 'disliked the black cap and the solemnity of moral verdicts.... [He] never discovered the principle by which conduct may be judged.... He enjoyed the luxury of indecision'[16].

A further and most important consequence follows from this contrast in impartiality. If Ranke did not know the principle by which conduct was to be judged, he obviously could not teach conduct. He had, Acton wrote, 'a low view of history. [He] disagrees about history emancipating'[17]. What was meant by this? How could history emancipate?

The answer is again to be found in the result of the process whereby 'certain' history is attained. For this certainty has the characteristic of being a search for the ideal that is conducted in the realm of the real. When the result of the search for the real, that is to say, all the gleanings of the romantic, are subsequently seen from the moral point of view they are in effect weighed against the latter. The historian inevitably becomes a judge – or, as Acton puts it: 'True impartiality ... judges resolutely'[18]. For Acton history had this paramount function of bringing into the closest possible juxtaposition the real and the ideal, thereby contributing to the transcendence of both. The task he ascribed to history was identical with that ascribed by a recent thinker to philosophy: 'It opposes the breach between ideas and reality. Philosophy confronts the existent, in its historical context, with the claims of its conceptual principles, in order to criticise the relation between the two and thus transcend them'[19].

Acton was himself aware of this relationship between history, as he conceived it, and philosophy conceived as criticism. Indeed, to Acton, it seems, any thinker who did not take the real as his *point de départ* but approached the real from the level of the ideal, working downwards, as it were, rather than upwards, would qualify as a critical philosopher. The essential criterion, was the position of the starting-point. His model in this respect was Plato – a not surprising choice in view of the latter's association in the creation of idealist philosophy. Those anti-Platonists who see in *The Republic*, for example, the consecration of the *status quo*, would have found no stronger opponent than Acton, even though he termed *The Republic* 'a fantastic dream' and 'a plea for despotism'. A paragraph from his review of Sir Erskine May's *Democracy in Europe* explains how and why he came to see in Plato the revolutionary implication of the ideal claim, looking 'downwards' at actuality: 'He [*i.e.* Plato] believed that no State can command obedience if it does not deserve respect; and he encouraged citizens to despise their government if they were not governed by wise men. . . . Plato would not suffer a democratic polity; but he challenged all existing authorities to justify themselves before a superior tribunal. . . . The prodigious vitality of his writings has kept the glaring perils of popular government constantly before mankind; but it has also preserved the belief in ideal politics and the notion of judging the powers of this world by a standard from heaven. There has been no fiercer enemy of democracy; but there has been no stronger advocate of revolution'[20]. A note makes the same point with equal clarity: 'The doctrine of ideas is the doctrine of Revolution. In comparing what is with what ought to be, Plato disclaims arbitrary invention. He sets his aim at the thought of God. He follows a Kingdom that exists in the ideal world'[21].

What Acton aimed at was to transport this comparison from the abstract sphere of philosophy into the concrete sphere of history. What was philosophically abstract would thereby become historically concrete. The two terms of the comparison would remain, but instead of their separation they would be brought into the closest possible juxtaposition. The 'notion of ideal politics' would be brought up against 'the powers of this world' with the maximum of emphasis.

What is the effect of this, within Acton's frame of reference? What relation do actualities bear to the ideal? Acton has himself answered the question in a passage from the early essay on 'Nationality' when he describes the imaginary state of the philosophers. 'Their commonwealth', he writes, 'is a satire as well as a model.' He had in mind such constructions as Plato's *Republic*, More's *Utopia* and Campanella's *City of the Sun*. Their ideal perfection constituted a satire on reality in that they incorporated 'those materials which were omitted from the fabric of the actual communities by the defects of which they were inspired'[22].

In the same way, history was a satire and the historian an inevitable satirist. As a moralist the historian is inspired by respect for human life with its embodiment in corresponding political and economic institutions and policies. But when he incorporates this inspiration in the actuality disclosed by his research, he cannot but become aware of an enormous discrepancy between the two. In this lies the origin of his satire. All that exists as real is a satire of its existence as ideal.

The satire results in a *spontaneous* criticism of reality. 'Let a man criminate himself' wrote Acton to Creighton[23]. In precisely the same way the world also condemned itself, with history making the condemnation articulate. Acton considerably weakens his own case when he suggests, in his comments on Ranke for example, that the historian actually puts on 'a black cap'. He is far truer to himself in writing that 'a man shall be condemned out of his *own* mouth'[24]. Furthermore, strictly speaking, the historian comes to no conclusion of his own accord. His conclusion is contained already in the juxtaposition of an evidence which is not of his own creation. Thus Acton can write: 'The historian does not conclude. The divine always concludes. Inconsistencies do not matter. He had not got to canonise or to sentence to the gallows.

As long as (the latter) two things are clear by evidence of history, he is content and asks no more'[25].

The historian asks no more, because he has already done all that he should or can do. In Marxist terminology, he has 'unmasked' the gap separating ideals from reality. Amongst Acton's notes there is an appreciative reference to 'that Greek philosophy which had dissolved Athens, which was feared, even in Socrates, asking the reason of things'[26]. In the same way, history also dissolved reality by 'asking the reason of things'. Rather, perhaps, the question emerged of its own accord when history showed 'the false morality of practical politics' [27]; or how often the great man was also a bad man; or not the 'glory' of war but 'the effects of wounds . . . the cannon wheels crashing over the bones of the wounded . . . the havoc wrought by a piece of shell tearing through the living trunk . . . the scenes in the hospitals, the ruined homes, the devastation'[28]. This was the sort of question that history asked of history. It put history to the test in 'asking the reason of things' – above all, in asking the reason for the unending desecration of human life.

History also did more. If it revealed the enormous gap separating the ideal from the real, if it was therefore the most truthful satire on human life conceivable, then it became in addition what Acton called 'a school of liberalism'. It showed, he writes, 'that three great things are not what they seem – Fame, antiquity and power. People rather like themselves – not better in proportion to greatness but worse'[29]. This theme, the disintegrating impact of historic truth, is expressed by Acton from all angles in numerous epigrams. He calls history 'an iconoclast – not a school, teacher of reverence. . . . The feet of many men, valued by divines, crumble to pieces in the contact with history'; or again – 'History undermines respect. Very little looking up to persons . . . wherein history is liberal, teaches disrespect. Shows up horrors, errors, follies, crimes of the ablest and the best. . . .'[30].

'History is not a master but a teacher', runs another of Acton's epigrams[31]. How and why should this be so? The unspoken assumption behind all Acton's theory of the task of history is the view that man cannot tolerate the reflection of his own degradation as held up to him in the mirror of history. He cannot stand the knowledge that his leaders are evil men; that his theories are mere illusions to justify his cruelty to others; that his social and economic arrangements violate every decree of humanity; that his wars are not glorious but a matter of devastation and ruined homes. In short he cannot stand the awareness that his actual life is but a satire of his life as it could, and ultimately will be.

It is in this way that the assertion of true morality effectively exposes the false morality of the world. History contains both the exposure and the means to redemption. It swells into a gigantic, sustained and unremitting criticism of the allegiances that bar the way to progress. But what is taken away with one hand, in the emancipation of man from the false idols of respect, obedience and tradition, is abundantly returned with the other. The truth sets man free but it does not leave him without guidance. Rather, the truth makes it possible to co-operate with providence in the path of progress. The choice remains with man – 'Knowledge of history means choice of ancestors'[32].

CHAPTER VII

A Comment

THE preceding chapters have been devoted to an examination of Acton's historical attitude. It has been shown that this can be reduced in essence to five main principles: *Romantik*, which sees its task in identification with the course of history itself; Liberalism, which views history from the standpoint of an extra-historical moral attitude; the contemporaneity of history when *Romantik* is overcome by Liberalism; the notion of progress as revolution, provoked by contemporaneity; and finally, the task of history in serving as the agent of progress.

What is to be said of this? To all appearances, Acton makes little or no attempt to deal with the obstacles that require to be overcome before his conclusions become visible, let alone attained. Acton's historical attitude raises well-nigh every question with which a philosophy of history has to grapple. Acton requires to show that one mind may come to know another mind; that the historical experience is not man's only experience of the world; that the past exists in its own right, independently of the present; that the universe opens on to a transcendent purpose; that any historian could attain simultaneously to the degree both of absolute sympathy and absolute detachment required. Entirely apart from the question whether Acton's prescription would actually *work*, these are but some of the propositions that he needs to show. There are innumerable others. As it is, none of them is even broached. So far as is ascertainable, Acton takes them all in his stride. But that he did not concern himself at all with the problems that he implicitly or explicitly raises is unlikely. All the evidence of his reading, notes, letters, etc, points the other way. Occasionally something of the kind is directly mentioned. For example, all the very wide embrace of the theory of morality with which Acton confronted Döllinger was not, Acton emphasises, 'a hasty paradox or prejudice'. On the contrary, his view, he said, was 'the result of many years' incessant study, and varied observation'[1]. But illumination of this kind is the exception – and even here the enlightenment concerns only the mere fact and not the detailed steps. Generally speaking, here as elsewhere, the reasoning behind the conclusions is not perceptible.

The effect of this is of course seriously to restrict the degree in which Acton's views may be assessed and critically examined. If the process of their formation is not visible, then it clearly cannot be possible to judge the finished product, except within wide limits. Where a thinker is concerned, the proof of the pudding is not in the eating but the cooking.

Nevertheless, too much should not be made of this objection. There would be nothing inherently unreasonable in the assumption that Acton's conclusions could step by step be intellectually justified. This is, on the contrary, more than likely when it is recalled that none of them, strictly speaking, can be said to be an original discovery. All have been maintained in one form or another by previous thinkers, who do indeed provide the foundations that are not to be found in Acton. Thus, if the latter's work contains views originally expressed by such a diversity of predecessors and contemporaries as Plato, Voltaire, Burke, Hegel, Schopenhauer, Marx and Dilthey, then it is here that the foundations must be sought and at the same time the justification for much that is fragmentary in Acton's work. The effect of these reflections is therefore to remove Acton from the ranks of those who express themselves in the form of brilliantly inspired *aperçus* and, even though his medium is informal and unlaboured, to give his work a well-founded basis.

If, in this way, the assumption may be made that Acton's views are inherently justifiable, and systematic, then certain conclusions follow. The first must obviously indicate that despite the heterogeneous nature of its origins, Acton's final scheme belongs undoubtedly to him alone. He is an original thinker in the sense that his originality does not lie in the separate components of his thought but rather in the manner in which he has brought together insights first enunciated by others and to some extent those 'in the air' in the second half of the nineteenth century. Nietzsche's conception of 'critical history' may serve as an example of this.

The combination of insights woven together by Acton has two aspects that must now be examined. Within its own premisses Acton's scheme – if the word for a moment be allowed – is, apart from one obvious gap to be examined below, an unshakable structure. As it stands, it cannot be refuted except by reference to a chain of reasoning that would overthrow the initial postulates. But once these are granted, then the system, with the qualification mentioned above, is internally consistent and a self-contained, self-enclosed whole. There is no internal contradiction. Each step in Acton's analysis of man and history is logically, if not empirically, connected with its predecessor. Step by step the scope of the analysis grows until, from a starting-point that shows man in history, the analysis swells gradually into a vision of man beyond history. The vision is important, grandiose and compelling.

The consistency and importance of the vision is paralleled by its strength. If a wider and deeper interest can be discerned today in Acton than was ever the case in his lifetime, then it is to his strength that this is attributable. This may well be the compensation for the intellectually isolated position occupied by Acton, in that he was prevented from succumbing to the complacency and illusion that overcame contemporary historians. At one level Acton may be included amongst those aristocratic sceptics of the nineteenth century, such as Burckhardt and Tocqueville, who saw all too clearly the totalitarian shape of things to come. Acton's perception of the connection between democracy and militarism, for example, and his vision of the future's 'great military monarchies' may well be set side by side with Burckhardt's vision of 'the military state [which] must become one great factory. Those hordes of men in the great industrial centres may not be left indefinitely to their greed and want. What must logically come is a definite and supervised stint of misery, with promotions and in uniforms, daily begun and ended to the sound of drums'[2]. At this level, Acton's interpretation of man and of the world can confront the test of time and emerge unscathed. Acton's message is opportune, all the more so as he was a genuine humanitarian and deeply sympathetic to the human claims embodied in the democratic urge, however much he might fear its final outcome.

There is also a yet deeper level, independent of changing political forms, that testifies to the strength of Acton's thought. Acton *can* confront the forced labour, concentration camps and gas-chambers of the twentieth century on the basis of his knowledge of previous society. To a man who identified the presence of the same evil in, for example, the slave trade, religious persecution, the Inquisition, political trials, war and conquest, the events of the twentieth century would only provide additional evidence *of the same kind* and not material for a complete revaluation of man. Acton's sense of outrage would grow; it would not have to come into being. He would know none of the sense of confusion that characterises the present-day intellect in the face of cruelty. He had seen so much of it before. He would be able to say, unlike the usual uncomprehending and bewildered liberal, that the twentieth century's multiplied manifestations of cruelty are by no means the result of man's technical capacities having outstripped his wisdom. Where, he would ask, is the evidence that this wisdom has ever manifested itself in action? Might it not be truer to ask whether technical advance was not at last bidding fair to allow full scope to the destructive tendencies in man? It is, indeed, only the type of person who sees as did Fisher in the Treaty of Utrecht, with its provision for the right to trade in slaves, 'a wise series of compromises' with 'no occasion for rancorous dispute' who can, on the one hand, be so easily reduced to agnostic despair, or, on the other, be forced to seek refuge in unreal dreams.

To those on the other flank who call for a religious revival, or a return to belief, or urge some other such formula, Acton would be able to reply with an identical question: had the ages of faith been more respectful of human life than ages of unbelief? Acton, with his doctrine of the contemporaneity of history would have been unable to admit any such differentiation. It is precisely because Acton stood outside the main schools and currents of the nineteenth-century intellectual world that he was able to disregard its optimism and, beneath the surface, to see both the transitory and the more enduring symptoms of instability.

Finally, the timeliness of Acton's appeal owes a great deal

to a certain intellectual austerity and nudity. He eschews all approach except the rigidly intellectual. His style is tense, dramatic, analytical, without artifice, image or colour. This is the medium corresponding to Acton's diagnosis – man and truth alone in the world. There are no other factors that might soften, as it were, this confrontation with the eternal. All is vanity, excepting truth. Man can put no faith in his leaders or the various doctrines that profess to lead along their various paths to the Promised Land. The first succumb inevitably to their position; the second are mere cloaks to justify the ill-treatment of others. These are the truths disclosed by history, from which alone man can draw encouragement. Beyond them there is nothing but illusion. This fearlessness in all its aspects might be said to form the backbone of Acton's present-day appeal. His is a strong and courageous doctrine that can withstand the onslaught of events.

So much for the positive side. What can be said on the negative? In accordance with the limits within which criticism can be profitably exercised, no attempt will be made to assess in detail Acton's historical attitude. Attention will exclusively be given to the pivot around which the remainder revolves – the notion of morality. This is not only central but is also elaborated to a greater degree than Acton's other concepts. Even so, it is here that 'the gap' already mentioned reveals itself as Acton's most startling weakness, the surmounting of which must be taken on trust if Acton's scheme is to be considered *en bloc*. There is of course no merit in consistency as such. On the contrary, it might well be the part of honesty to admit if necessary an inability to reconcile two contradictory insights both of which are thought to be true rather than impose a superficial pattern of conformity. But the gap in question is not of this kind. It concerns the virtually complete absence of any discussion by Acton of the relationship between the individual and the collective. Acton speaks of the collective redemption of man, yet his morality deals with the individual. In other words, can Acton's view of morality bear the burden he imposes on it? It clearly cannot. Furthermore, although there is no doubt that he himself was aware of this disparity, there is just as little doubt that he shied away from its examination. The consequences would have been too devastating to his excessively simple view of the world.

Here no attempted solution will be propounded to the problem: if for no other reason it would lead too far beyond our present scope. We merely wish to show the inadequacies of Acton's own moral view. Why can it not act as the criterion for which it is intended? Why can it not become a basis for the historian's judgment?[3]

To show why this is so, it is necessary to examine the presuppositions of Acton's world. Broadly speaking, free-will is its dominating characteristic. Were this not the case, there could be no question of moral responsibility. If man is not free to choose right or wrong, then there is as little merit in choosing the first as culpability in choosing the second. Acton is obliged to presuppose a world of freely-willing individuals. Furthermore, these individuals have an additional characteristic in that they are *unattached*. They have no existence in reality but live in a social and political vacuum. No matter in what position they find themselves, they are abstracted from it and confronted with a fellow-man who is similarly conceived in the abstract. Whether it is Napoleon or the humblest conscript of the *Grande Armée*, the Pope or a parish priest, a Foreign Secretary or the lowliest dispatch clerk, all are withdrawn from their immediate circumstances and confronted, on the one hand, with their neighbour and, on the other hand, with the demands of morality. This mass of individuals is free to obey or disobey the demands. If they choose to disobey, nothing but their own ill-will can be held responsible. If they choose to obey, then this is again entirely due to their goodwill. Acton's morality makes no sense at all if it does not presuppose that what happens in any given situation is the result of any number of individually free choices.

Does this view correspond to the facts of social and political life? Can an individual be abstracted from his environment in this way? It is not necessary to examine very closely the relationship between the individual and the group to see that the result of this procedure is an unreal entity, above all where moral claims are concerned. It is for this reason that many of Acton's judgments give the effect of being extracts from *1066 and All That*. They irresistibly recall judgments such as 'King John was a bad king' and 'King Richard was a good king'. What Acton does is to neglect almost entirely the influences of the groups to which Kings John and Richard respectively belonged in determining the moral nature of their activity. He does not of course exempt their groups, or any other historical association for that matter, such as church, nation or party, from moral concern. On the contrary, these, like any individual, are all subordinate to the same idea. But it is the crucial area of intersection that is left unexplored. This is the area where the abstract unreal individual actually comes into existence as a participant in history and in this capacity susceptible to moral assessment.

Without it being necessary in any way to diminish Acton's conception of responsibility where group existence is concerned, it is not possible to transfer to this complex sphere the simple scheme of a morality conceived in purely personal, inter-individual terms. As a matter of fact, the obligation, for example, to respect one's neighbour's life is itself misconceived in relation to its object for the capacity in which two 'neighbours' encounter each other is not an individual capacity, but they do and can only meet in so far as both are members of certain groups. And it is this membership that will either hinder or facilitate, make possible or impossible, the obligation of mutual respect. If the moral obligation is thus misconceived on an individual scale, how much more must this be the case when the obligation is transferred unchanged to a far larger and more complex sphere? Acton errs not only in conceiving the moral object to be the individual but also in applying this misconception to a group-sphere distinct from the individual or any sum of its constituent individuals.

The problem can be illustrated from its occasional appearances in Acton's own works. Take, for example, the socialist. As member of an ideological or political group he is, although inspired by the hope of freedom, in actual fact helping to inaugurate the loss of freedom. He is helping to create a situation that is very much opposed to his own willing, although it is also very much of his own doing. In so far as he is to be judged by *results* and not intention, then Acton's morality can justly condemn both him and his group. But the morality has no verdict to give when it is appreciated that the conduct of the socialist has been substantially modified by the fact of his acting in a certain way in regard to a certain group. What is essential here, and what is omitted by Acton, is the modification undergone by a man's conduct on his adhering to the socialist group. It is not the assessment of his attributes as an individual that is at stake but the essentially new that is added and created by the adherence.

The same conflict is involved in an early review by Acton

of Emile Augier's anti-clerical play *Le Fils de Giboyer*. He reproaches the author for a simplification of the central situation of his play. Augier, writes Acton, does not show the alliance between the Church and a reactionary aristocracy 'in all the tragic magnitude of its evil'. This 'unnatural conjuncture', he emphasises, has not arisen as the result of 'sensuality and conscious hypocrisy' on the part of the clergy. It is a question of 'perverting the sense of right'[4]. In other words, the point is blurred and falsified if conscious ill-will is attributed to a process that transcends the individual's willing in its association with a group.

That Acton was obscurely aware of the inadequacy of his moral analysis seems very likely. The more he insists on the guilt of individuals, the more his intensity seems intended to dispel certain doubts concerning the judgment's validity. As it was, however, these doubts had the effect of inclining him from one extreme to the other. From extreme individualism he swung over to an equally extreme supra-individualism. Thus on one occasion he produced a note in astonishing contrast to the body of his thought: 'History deals with impersonal forces. It does not condescend to individual conduct. Hanging is a biographical incident that has nothing to do with the roll of the ages. The science of meteorology is not conversant with the qualities of seamen'[5]. In its assumption of a historical process pursuing its way heedless of the passions and puny exertions of men, treating them with sublime indifference, this represents a complete reversal of the Acton whose 'microscopic interests' would so overwhelmingly have held up 'the majestic march of civilisation'. It is Acton's version of the Hegelian assumption that the course of world history lies beyond good and evil.

It is, of course, an extreme statement for Acton to make. Generally speaking, the embarrassment in which he occasionally found himself, if it has been correctly identified as such, found expression in shying away from the perplexity. He had, it appears, an evident distaste for any system that explained human activity in any terms other than the individualist terms of personal willing and acting. Thinkers as disparate as Gobineau and Darwin come under the same attack. The former's 'doctrine of Race' is described as 'one of many schemes to deny free-will, responsibility and guilt and to supplant moral by physical causes'. The latter, by insisting on the influence of surroundings, 'strengthens the view that man depends on them'[6]. In the same spirit Acton drew up a lengthy list which he headed: 'Negations of Free Will' – 'Heredity, Race, Climate, Evolution, Positivism, Socialism, Democracy, Pantheism, Success, Necessity, Survival'[7]. In 'Sociology' Acton saw the same 'reduction of the personal element'[8].

Other examples of the same kind could be given. Their effect is always to confirm Acton's reluctance to depart from his naïve, simplified view of human behaviour. Whether or not he was aware of it, he too had 'a magic wand'. If Hegel's 'magic wand' explained away too much by the action of *impersonal* forces, then Acton's explained too much in the terms of *personal* forces. If Augier over-simplified the tiny situation with which he dealt, then Acton is similarly unsatisfying and inadequate on an enormously larger scale. In both cases the problem is masked and its solution thereby jeopardised.

If this is taken as *the* problem that Acton's morality raises, and the comprehensive embrace of morality left unexamined, the corresponding implication is the latter's justification; that is, in principle, for Acton was not an absolutist or a perfectionist. This would have removed him for ever to the sphere of futility. His intention was undoubtedly to draw up a cast-iron scheme which would infallibly supply the answer to any moral predicament. The phrase – 'the science' – be it of morality or politics, means no less. It was meant to convey the existence of a book of rules, reference to which would solve every difficulty of life. As it happened, Acton was not able to force the manifold variety of life into cast-iron categories of conduct. It is sufficient to note in this respect his quotation – 'the Sabbath is made for man, not man for the Sabbath'[9]. Besides, Acton, more perhaps than any other revolutionary, could not but realise that he was working with poor – though not inadequate – material. It is not a question of making allowances for human weakness but of not setting the impossibly high standard of the perfectionist. Otherwise, once again, Acton would have condemned himself to futility. He would have condemned himself to becoming that sort of utopian whose hopes are quite unconnected with reality. Therefore, if these questions be bluntly put: is it possible to treat human life with the universal respect he demanded? Is it possible to require from the world this recognition? – the answer must be an equally blunt 'no'. Acton was not an absolute pacifist as would necessarily have followed from his acceptance of the unconditional sanctity of human life. He was his own *advocatus diaboli*. These are words he puts into the mouth of Machiavelli, his antithesis: 'The force of evil is such in this world that it would prevail if virtue tied its hands with scruples – if evil had the monopoly of the most efficient means – if virtue disarms before the engagement – if one thinks only of the end, the other only of the means'[10]. For obvious reasons, Acton does not make much of specific historical cases where virtue, lest it be forcibly exterminated by evil, might forcibly resist evil. He was above all anxious not to open the slightest loophole wherein adversaries might insert a Torquemada or a Robespierre. Yet scattered here and there is mention of the right to 'resistance'. Acton regretted that Socrates 'gave no warrant to resistance. He emancipated men for thought, but not for action'[11]. Again, Acton also sympathised with 'Jewish resistance' to Syrian and Roman persecution[12].

There is not much more in this strain that might be unambiguously added. But of course enough has been said to make a breach in Acton's scheme of morality. How far does the breach extend? Does it go so far as to rank him, willy-nilly, with those who claim that the social and individual order is inherently incapable of being subjected to the scheme? The difference appears to be one of emphasis. But in actual fact there is all the difference in the world between those who make exceptions to a rule and those who make a rule of the exceptions. In justification of his revolt against the experience of history Acton might echo Kant: 'That the actions of man will never be in perfect accordance with all the requirements of the pure idea of reason, does not prove the thought to be chimerical. For only through this idea are all judgments as to moral merit or demerit possible; it consequently lies at the foundation of every approach to moral perfection, however far removed from it the obstacles in human nature – indeterminable as to degree – may keep us . . . in relation to ethical laws experience is the parent of illusion, and it is in the highest degree reprehensible to limit or to deduce the laws which dictate *I ought to do*, from *what is done*'[13].

APPENDIX

Acton and the American Revolution

AT VARIOUS points in the preceding chapters it has been shown how the urge to act occasionally introduced into Acton's thought and conduct elements of utopianism. It emerged in his abortive diplomatic career for example, and it also threatened to emerge in his treatment of the French Revolution. Acton could not support Gladstone, or ask him for a post in the Cabinet, or suggest that he represent the British Government in Munich and *at the same time* continue to hold the political views that he did. He might, of course, have made a moral distinction between, say, Gladstone and Disraeli, but it could not be absolute. Acton could not see 'fulfilled' in Gladstone, as he is reported to have done, 'the idea that politics is an affair of morality, that it touches eternal interests and eternal standards as much as vices and virtues in private life'[1]. How could a hyperion remain a hyperion – and yet work through the same institutions as a satyr?

This suppressed undercurrent of emotionalism only burst through in full spate in Acton's treatment of the American Revolution. He welcomed 1776 in rhetorical and exalted terms, quite at variance with his usual prosaic style. 'The story of the revolted colonies', he wrote, 'impresses us first and most distinctly as the supreme manifestation of the law of resistance, as the abstract revolution in its purest and most perfect shape . . . it teaches us that men ought to be in arms even against a remote and constructive danger to their freedom; that even if the cloud is no bigger than a man's hand, it is their right and duty to stake the national existence, to sacrifice lives and fortunes, to cover the country with a lake of blood, to shatter crowns and sceptres and fling parliaments into the sea. On this principle of subversion they [*i.e.* the American revolutionaries] erected their commonwealth, and by its virtue lifted the world out of its orbit and assigned a new course to history. Here or nowhere we have the broken chain, the rejected past, precedent and statute superseded by unwritten law, sons wiser than their fathers, ideas rooted in the future, reason cutting as clean as Atropos'[2].

This dithyrambic assertion is no preparation at all for the calm tones in which the American Constitution of 1787 is discussed. Here the talk is of 'eminently cautious and sensible men', 'when every effort was made, every scheme was invented, to curb the inevitable democracy'[3]. Why should this caution be necessary? Surely the inescapable implication is that the victory of the idea – 'reason cutting as clean as Atropos' – is incompatible with the reign of liberty, in the name of which the Revolution is undertaken. The contradiction has been identified as 'a dilemma' encompassing Acton's political philosophy. 'If liberty', one of his critics has written, 'depends upon an institutional framework in which a neutral mechanism of checks and balances expresses and resolves the clash of social forces, it cannot also depend upon the absolute triumph of a single moral idea. In the first place liberty is conceived in a spirit of limitation, of limited ends and limited means, conservative suspicion and caution, compromises and expedients. . . . In the second case liberty is characterised as the impulse of a daring idea projected along a course of action possibly terminating in revolution:

it is satisfied with nothing less than the reign of conscience, an absolute and universal morality admitting neither compromise nor caution'[4].

What is the explanation? Why did Acton exempt the American revolutionaries from every stricture which he passed elsewhere on political action of this type? Why was Danton not even allowed a reign of terror if the Americans were allowed to cover their country with 'a lake of blood'? Again, if reason in 1776 'cut as clean as Atropos', how was it possible that a historical phenomenon such as slavery should make its appearance on American soil?

The explanation of the 'dilemma' seems to lie in a confusion in Acton's mind. Perhaps because America was so far away, he succumbed to the illusion that there had been the site of the ideal revolution. But in actual fact, he located the ideal in the real. And this true contradiction arose not from his political philosophy but from his character. The position of constant critic that he occupied was not always equal to the burden that he thereby imposed upon himself. For the person insensitive to suffering, the strain would hardly have existed, if at all. For a person so sensitive to suffering as was Acton, and of such humanitarian instinct, the strain was at times intolerable. It is not unnatural, therefore, that he sometimes saw a light where none existed, that he confused the two levels in his thought and located the ideal in the real. Acton's support of the American Revolution is more of a tribute to his heart than to his head. The hyperbolical terminology alone indicates the emotional factors at work[5].

it is satisfied with nothing less than the reign of conscience, an absolute and universal morality admitting neither compromise nor caution".

What is the explanation? Why did Acton exempt the American revolutionaries from every stricture which he passed elsewhere on political action of this type? Why was he not even allowed a reign of terror if the Americans were allowed to cover their country with a lake of blood? What reason is there to declare that Acton, how was it tolerable that a monstrous phenomenon such as slavery should in the end disappear? Nor can we ask.

The explanation of this dilemma seems to be in a confusion in Acton's mind. Perhaps because America was so far away, he succumbed to the illusion that there had been the one of the ideal revolution. But in actual fact, he located the ideal in the real. And this true contradiction arose not from his political philosophy but from his character. The position in concert with what he complained is not always equal to the burden that he thereby imposed upon himself. For the person insensitive to suffering, the strain would hardly have existed; but for a person so sensitive to suffering as was Acton, and of such humanitarian instinct, the strain was at times intolerable. It is not unnatural, therefore, that he sometimes saw a light where none existed, that he confused the two levels of his thought and located the ideal in the real. Acton's support of the American Revolution is more of a tribute to his heart than to his head. The hyperbolical terminology alone indicates the emotional factors at work".

NOTES

NOTE ON METHOD

[1] Add. MSS. 4865.

[2] H. J. Morgenthau, *Scientific Man versus Power Politics*, p. 168, London 1947.

[3] *E.g.* in Dr G. P. Gooch's 'Lord Acton: Apostle of Liberty' (*Foreign Affairs*, July 1947) and in Professor E. L. Woodward's 'The Place of Lord Acton in the Liberal Movement of the Nineteenth Century' (*Politica*, September 1939).

[4] They are here referred to as Add. MSS.

INTRODUCTION

[1] H. A. L. Fisher, *Studies in History and Politics*, p. 86, Oxford 1920. The quotation is taken from a review of Acton's works that originally appeared in 1911.

[2] *S.C.* p. 195.

[3] *Autobiography of Edward Gibbon*, Everyman edition, pp. 12-13 and 19.

[4] *S.C.* pp. 1-2.

[5] This letter is quoted by Lady Blennerhassett in her obituary of Acton in the *Deutsche Rundschau* of January 1905. The letter was originally written in French – the language in which Acton and his mother usually conversed and corresponded. For the purpose of her obituary Lady Blennerhassett translated it into German, whence the extracts quoted have been rendered into English.

[6] *Ibid*. The same remarks apply to this letter as to the foregoing.

[7] *S.C.* p. 8. Figgis and Lawrence, the editors of Acton's correspondence, wrongly date this letter 1848. It can only have originated in 1850, for it refers also to Döllinger's presence at the Bavarian Assembly which met in the summer of that year.

[8] *S.C.* p. 26.

[9] The mission to Moscow was led by Granville. It had the dual purpose of smoothing over Anglo-Russian relations after the

Crimean War and of representing Queen Victoria at the coronation of the new Czar Alexander II. Acton's role was that of a sort of secretary to the mission. A not unhumorous record exists of his diplomatic activity. The 'Order Book of the British Embassy – Moscow 1856', preserved amongst the Acton papers, contains this note in Acton's hand. It bears the date September 16, 1856, and runs: 'It is particularly requested that the members of the Embassy will for some days at least be punctual at breakfast. In consequence of the preparations for the ball the room will be occupied by workmen all day excepting their dinner hour, from 11 to 12. It will therefore be impossible to have breakfast served after 12 o'clock. Q.E.D.

By order.

J. D. Acton' (Add. MSS. 4872)

[10] Add. MSS. 5528. A letter of May 1854 to Granville has the same purport though the sentiment is not expressed so explicitly (*S.C.* pp. 26-27).

[11] *Home and Foreign Review*, p. 163, July 1863.

[12] Add. MSS. 5020.

[13] *L.A.C.* p. 1. It was typical of Acton's self-confidence, not to say bumptiousness, at this time, that he could write in an early notebook: 'We who have a Wiseman to govern us, a Faber to preach to us, and a Newman to think for us, must be all right, seems to be a popular idea' (Add. MSS. 5528).

[14] *Home and Foreign Review*, pp. 512-517, October 1862; see also Acton's article 'The Catholic Press' in *The Rambler*, February 1859.

[15] *The Rambler*, pp. 73-74, February 1859.

[16] *The Rambler*, p. 174, January 1861. Baur was the founder of the Tübingen school and flourished in the mid-nineteenth century. David Friedrich Strauss, whose *Das Leben Jesu* denied the divinity of Christ, was one of his pupils.

[17] Dr G. P. Gooch, *History and Historians in the Nineteenth Century*, p. 382, London 1913.

[18] The speech is quoted at length in Acton's reply to the Cardinal, originally published in the *Home and Foreign Review* and reprinted *H.O.F.* pp. 436 ff.

[19] *L.A.C.* pp. 317-318. Simpson was a convert and the author of a noted biography of Campion, the English Jesuit.

[20] *H.O.F.* p. 489.

[21] For the details of Acton's Parliamentary career, see James J. Auchmuty, 'Acton's Election as an Irish Member of Parliament' in the *English Historical Review*, vol. LXI, 1946. As a member of the House of Lords – he was raised to the peerage on Gladstone's recommendation in 1869 – Acton took the same virtually silent course that he had taken in the Lower House.

[22] Lord Edmond Fitzmaurice, *Life of the 2nd Earl Granville*, vol. I, p. 262, London 1905.

[23] *S.C.* p. 28.

[24] *L.A.C.* pp. 155-156, pp. 190-191. 'Nationality', perhaps Acton's most frequently quoted article, appeared in the *Home and Foreign Review* in 1862.

[25] The Count Arco-Valley who assassinated Kurt Eisner, one of the leaders of the Bavarian Soviet Republic in 1919, was a member of the same family.

[26] Add. MSS. 4862.

[27] Add. MSS. 5645.

[28] *The Chronicle*, pp. 369-370, 13th July 1867.

[29] *S.C.* p. 91.

[30] See 'Quirinus', *Letters from Rome on the Council*, Authorised English translation, London 1870.

[31] Lord Acton, *Sendschreiben an einen deutschen Bischof des Vatikanischen Concils*, p. 1, Nördlingen, September 1870.

[32] Add. MSS. 4912.

[33] This letter is reprinted in *S.C.* pp. 124 ff.

[34] Add. MSS. 4905.

[35] Add. MSS. 5502, 5512.

[36] Add. MSS. 5019. Acton does not specifically state that he is here referring to himself but there can be no doubt that this is the case.

[37] *S.C.* p. 185.

[38] Sir Mountstuart Grant Duff, *Out of the Past*, pp. 191-192, London 1903.

[39] *Ibid*, p. 188.

[40] See Lady Blennerhassett's obituary of Acton in *Deutsche Rundschau*, January 1905.

[41] See the article by the late R. A. L. Smith on Acton in the *New Statesman*, vol. XXVII, No. 692.

[42] See Acton's letter to Creighton of 14th August 1885 in Add. MSS. 6871.

[43] Add. MSS. 4945.

[44] Add. MSS. 5008, 5020, 5525.

[45] Add. MSS. 5403.

[46] Add. MSS. 5525. In the same pessimistic strain runs a quotation from Musset: '*Un souvenir heureux est peut-être sur terre Plus vrai que le bonheur*' (Add. MSS. 5629).

[47] David Ogg, *Herbert Fisher*, p. 172, London 1947.

[48] Add. MSS. 44094 (British Museum). Letter dated 1st October 1892.

[49] That is, if such a psychological curiosity as a notebook, its lines numbered up to 11,000 with here and there a title inserted, be excepted (Add. MSS. 4867).

[50] *L.M.G.* p. 100. The allusion is to Henry James' story of a painter who dedicated his life to the painting of a masterpiece. On his death the easel was found bare. The same joke recurred later when Acton wrote that the Cambridge Modern History was to be 'a whole choir of Madonnas' (*L.M.G.* p. 197).

[51] Add. MSS. 5645, 5684.

[52] *S.C.* p. ix.

[53] Add. MSS. 6171.

[54] *S.C.* p. 181. The italics have been added.

[55] Add. MSS. 5504.

[56] *L.M.G.* (1) pp. 174-175.

[57] *Edinburgh Review*, p. 531, April 1903.

[58] This phrase occurs in a letter to Creighton and refers to Acton's review of Döllinger's historical work.

[59] Add. MSS. 5690. The list is mainly of German writers. It includes Arndt, Becker, Schleiermacher, Dahlmann, Grimm, Gervinus, Döllinger, Höffler, Rotteck, Mohl. It is not clear why all these should be considered 'persecuted'. On the other hand, Döllinger was excommunicated; Rotteck's *Universalgeschichte* was placed on the Index and banned in Austria; and Gervinus, Dahlmann and the brothers Grimm were in 1837 deprived of their posts at the University of Göttingen when they publicly protested at the abrogation of the constitution.

[60] All these quotations are taken from the Acton-Creighton

correspondence Add. MSS. 6871. The italics have everywhere been added.

[61] Add. MSS. 4953.

[62] John Viscount Morley, *Recollections*, vol. I, p. 231, London 1924.

[63] *Life and Letters of Mandell Creighton* by his wife, vol. I, pp. 229, 370, London 1913.

[64] *S.C.* p. 297.

[65] It has elsewhere been pointed out that there are 'discrepancies' between Acton's notes and his lectures, and that when the two are compared it is usually the latter that 'ring false'. (See the article by Gertrude Himmelfarb, 'The American Revolution in the Political Theory of Lord Acton' in *Journal of Modern History* (Chicago), vol. XXI No. 4, December 1949.) The following examples are instructive. In his Inaugural Lecture at Cambridge (1895) Acton spoke with qualified approval of impartiality in these terms: 'If men were truly sincere, and delivered judgment by no canons but those of evident morality, then Julian would be described in the same terms by Christian and pagan, Luther by Catholic and Protestant, Washington by Whig and Tory, Napoleon by patriotic Frenchman and patriotic German' (*L.M.H.* pp. 17-18). Compare this with the equivalent formulation in a note: 'If a pagan and a Christian differ on the character of Julian; a Protestant and a Catholic on Luther; an Anglican and a Puritan on Calvin; a Frenchman and an Englishman on Napoleon – then one of the two is a liar' (Add. MSS. 4909). Again, in the Inaugural Acton spoke as follows of the value of letters to the historian: '... Hundreds and even thousands of the moderns have borne testimony against themselves, and may be studied in their private correspondence and sentenced, on their own confession' (*L.M.H.* p. 7). This is how a note voices the same sentiment: 'The modern can generally be hanged out of his own mouth' (Add. MSS. 5600). Sometimes the connection is not so close, as here for example. To Mary Gladstone Acton wrote of her father's oratorical skill: '... that illustrious chain of English eloquence that begins in the Napoleon battles, ends with Mr Gladstone ... he alone possesses all the qualities of an orator; and when men come to remember what his speeches accomplished, how it was the same whether he

prepared an oration or hurled a reply, whether he addressed a British mob or the cream of Italian politicians, and would still be the same if he spoke in Latin to Convocation, they will admit no rival' (*L.M.G.* p. 36). As compared with this, the tone of a note on the same subject of political oratory is quite otherwise: 'Effects of eloquence good to put down the red flag, or to obtain the unanimous war votes of a united parliament' (Add. MSS. 4929). Another distinction is that Acton tended to optimism in public and to pessimism in private. It was not for nothing that Acton doubted whether 'it would be possible for an honest historian to have a friend' (*L.F.R.* p. 373).

[66] *Cambridge Review*, 16th October 1902. This was not at the time the doubtful compliment that it has since become.

[67] James Bryce, *Studies in Contemporary Biography*, p. 387, London 1903.

[68] John Viscount Morley, *Recollections*, vol. I, p, 230, London 1924.

[69] Mountstuart Grant Duff, *op. cit.* pp. 192-193.

[70] The list is given, together with Acton's introductory comments, in C. K. Shorter's *Immortal Memories*, London 1907.

[71] Add. MSS. 4909.

[72] See above p. 20.

[73] *L.M.H.* pp. 21-22.

[74] Renan, *Essais de Morale et de Critique*, pp. 104-5, 2nd edition, Paris 1860.

[75] H. Butterfield, *The Whig Interpretation of History*, p.v., London 1950.

CHAPTER I

[1] *L.A.C.* p. 60.

[2] Add. MSS. 44093 (British Museum). Letter dated 30th June 1862.

[3] *L.M.G.* p. 187.

[4] *L.A.C.* p. 4.

[5] *E.g.* see p. 49.

[6] *L.A.C.* p. 124; *cf.* Burke's 'A state without the means of some change is without the means of its conservation' (*Reflections on the Revolution in France*).

[7] *H.O.F.* p. 243; *cf.* Burke's: 'The science of constructing a

commonwealth, or renovating it, or reforming it, is, like every other experimental science, not to be taught *a priori*.... The science of government being therefore so practical in itself... it is with infinite caution that any man ought to venture upon pulling down an edifice which has answered in any tolerable degree for ages the common purposes of society....' (*Reflections on the Revolution in France*).

[8] *H.O.F.* p. 280.

[9] *H.O.F.* pp. 276, 298.

[10] *The Rambler*, p. 397, March 1860.

[11] *Home and Foreign Review*, p. 314, January 1864.

[12] Crane Brinton, *English Political Thought in the Nineteenth Century*, p. 205, 2nd edition, London 1949.

[13] *F.A.P.* p. 246.

[14] *Ibid*, p. 250.

[15] *The Chronicle*, p. 139, 4th May 1867.

[16] *Home and Foreign Review*, p. 321, July 1863. The quotation is taken by Acton from the book under review at the time, Bonamy Price's, *Venetia and the Quadrilateral*.

[17] *The Chronicle*, p. 42, 11th January 1868.

[18] *The Chronicle*, p. 572, 7th September 1867. Baumgarten's *Wie wir wieder ein Volk geworden sind*, published on the eve of the establishment of the German Empire in 1871, received similar treatment: 'a hurried production written to satisfy a patriotic emotion rather than to satisfy a craving for historical science' (*North British Review*, p. 598, January 1871).

[19] *Home and Foreign Review*, p. 243, January 1863.

[20] *North British Review*, p. 275, October 1870. Acton's comment on a certain M. Bonhomme is worth quoting for its own sake no less than as an example of his arrogance. He describes Bonhomme as 'one of those useful Frenchmen who apply a very limited portion of literary power to the elucidation of proportionately minute details of history' (*Home and Foreign Review*, p. 631, April 1863).

[21] *The Chronicle*, p. 443, 3rd August 1867.

[22] *The Rambler*, p. 268, April 1858.

[23] *L.A.C.* p. 40.

[24] *H.O.F.* p. 324; *cf*. also the following passage from Acton's review of Goldwin Smith's *Irish History*: 'Intolerance... is a

political necessity against all religions which threaten the unity of faith in a state that is not free, and in every state against those religions which threaten its existence. Absolute intolerance belongs to the absolute state; special persecution may be justified by special causes in any state. All medieval persecution is of the latter kind, for the sects against which it was directed were revolutionary parties. The state really defended, not its religious unity, but its political existence' (*H.O.F.* p. 254).

[25] *H.O.F.* pp. 169-170. On the other hand, Acton also pointed out that persecution as such did not require the sanction of political situation: 'To say that persecution is wrong, nakedly, seems to me first of all untrue, but at the same time it is in contradiction with solemn decrees, with Leo X's Bull against Luther, with a Breve of Benedict XIV of 1748 and with one of Pius VI 1791' (*L.A.C.* p. 243). Acton also censured a certain H. Formby who, in a children's book entitled *Pictorial Bible and Church History Series* omitted this very aspect: '. . . he (*i.e.* Formby) tells us that the Albigenses were not only heretics but also 'the mischievous authors of a political disunion, which it concerned the general good of the Christian people to put down without loss of time by the force of arms. *Hence* an armed crusade against the *rebels* was proclaimed'. Now the author of an ecclesiastical history cannot be ignorant that the Holy See has held and practised the doctrine, that even where there was no civil rebellion, no danger to the public peace, and no possibility of propagating error, a heretic might be rightly put to death. . . . When the principle of persecution is considered, the Spanish Inquisition must be set aside: the crucial instance is the Inquisition in Rome, where the civil and spiritual powers were united, from the reign of Paul III to that of Clement VIII. We do not quarrel in the abstract with either the advocates or the enemies of toleration; but we cannot help thinking that Mr Formby has failed to bring his theory of persecution into harmony with his theory of authority' (*Home and Foreign Review*, pp. 218-219, January 1863). The italics in the passage quoted from Formby are Acton's. Paul III was Pope from 1534-1549, and Clement VIII from 1592-1605.

[26] Add. MSS. 5751.

[27] *H.O.F.* pp. 234-235.

[28] Add MSS. 5752.

[29] *H.E.S.* pp. 193-194. The italics have been added.

[30] *Home and Foreign Review*, p. 180, July 1863.

[31] *Ibid*, p. 152, January 1863.

[32] *The Chronicle*, pp. 31-32, 11th January, 1868.

[33] *The Chronicle*, p. 394, 20th July, 1867.

[34] *Home and Foreign Review*, p. 255, January 1863; *cf.* also 'The fourth volume of Mr Massey's History of the Reign of George III ... exhibits a stronger grasp of principle, a more confident *though* still impartial judgment, and deeper convictions, than the volumes which preceded it' (*Ibid*, p. 312, July 1863. The italics have been added).

[35] H. A. L. Fisher, *op. cit.* p. 91.

[36] Herbert Butterfield, *Lord Acton*, p. 9, London 1948.

CHAPTER II

[1] Add. MSS. 5684.

[2] Add. MSS. 4938.

[3] *L.M.H.* pp. 21-22.

[4] Add. MSS. 5478 and 5675.

[5] Add. MSS. 5478.

[6] *L.M.H.* pp. 24-25.

[7] Add. MSS. 5478. The italicised phrase is in the original.

[8] *Ibid.*

[9] *Ibid.*

[10] Add. MSS. 4994. Wilhelm Dilthey (1833-1911) was a German philosopher, literary critic and historian. One of his main interests was the detailed analysis of the process of *understanding*, as a means of becoming aware of our own mental life and that of others. Of Dilthey's major works Acton only knew *Das Leben Schleiermacher* (1867-70) and *Einleitung in die Geisteswissenschaften* (1883). All the others were published after Acton's death in 1902. It is of course not known whether, in view of their acquaintance, Acton may not have been able to discuss with Dilthey the development of his ideas.

[11] See pp. 40, ff.

[12] W. Dilthey, *Gesammelte Schriften*, vol. VII, p. 173, quoted and translated Hodges, *Wilhelm Dilthey – An Introduction*, p. 147, London 1944.

[13] Add. MSS. 5394.

[14] Add. MSS. 4905.

[15] Add. MSS. 5437, 5675, 5457, 5644.

[16] Add. MSS. 5467, 5684, 5509, 4991. Joubert, the French nineteenth century philosopher, is quoted to much the same effect: '*Il faut savoir entrer dans les idées des autres et savoir en sortir, comme il faut savoir sortir des siennes et y rentrer.*' (Add. MSS. 5454.)

[17] *L.M.G.* pp. 46-47. This may be usefully compared with Collingwood's statement of the relationship between the novelist and the historian: 'Each of them makes it his business to construct a picture which is partly a narrative of events, partly a description of situations, exhibition of motives, analysis of characters. Each aims at making his picture a coherent whole, where every character and every situation is so bound up with the rest that this character in this situation cannot but act in this way, and we cannot imagine him as acting otherwise. The novel and the history must both of them make sense and nothing is admissible in either except what is necessary....' (R. G. Collingwood, *The Historical Imagination*, pp. 17-18, Oxford 1935.)

[18] The full quotation runs as follows. It is to be found in Add. MSS. 5002: '*In der Ausdehnung auf die historischen Probleme meinte der Positivismus seinen entschiedenen Triumph zu feiern; an ihnen muss er zu Falle kommen*'. Wilhelm Windelband (1848-1915), best known as a German historian of philosophy. In his own thought he attempted to distinguish between the aims and methods of science and history.

[19] Add. MSS. 4861.

[20] Add. MSS. 5457.

[21] Add. MSS. 5470.

[22] Add. MSS. 5437.

[23] *L.M.H.* p. 22.

[24] Karl Löwith, *Meaning in History*, Introduction, Note 1, p. 225, Chicago 1949.

[25] This is the thesis argued in Theodor Lessing's *Geschichte als Sinngebung des Sinnlosen*, Munich 1919. It has recently been closely echoed: 'History is "true" only in so far as it is the reflection of the past in the mirror of the writer's personality'

(David Ogg, *Herbert Fisher*, p. 176, London 1947). This definition of historical truth would not exclude Hitler's *Mein Kampf*.

[26] Add. MSS. 5604.

[27] Add. MSS. 5478.

[28] Add. MSS. 5661.

CHAPTER III

[1] Add. MSS. 5684. To Creighton Acton wrote in similar terms: 'Good and evil lie close together. Seek no artistic unity in character' (Add. MSS. 6871).

[2] *L.M.H.* p. 27.

[3] Add. MSS. 6871.

[4] *Cf.* also: 'among all the causes which degrade and demoralise men, power is the most constant and the most active' (Add. MSS. 5611); and '. . . the possession of absolute power which corrodes the conscience, hardens the heart, and confounds the understanding of monarchs' (*H.O.F.* p. 11).

[5] *L.F.R.* p. 108.

[6] *L.M.G.* pp. 71-72.

[7] Add. MSS. 4941.

[8] Add. MSS. 5017 and 4862.

[9] *L.M.G.* p. 179.

[10] Add. MSS. 6871.

[11] Add. MSS. 5604.

[12] Add. MSS. 5020.

[13] Add. MSS. 6871. Barrow, Baxter and Bossuet were respectively a seventeenth century Protestant, Puritan and Catholic.

[14] Add. MSS. 5516.

[15] Add. MSS. 5432.

[16] *H.E.S.* pp. 494-495.

[17] *S.C.* p. 281.

[18] Add. MSS. 6871.

[19] Add. MSS. 6871.

[20] *H.O.F.* p. 205.

[21] See *H.E.S.* pp. 494-495.

[22] *L.M.G.* p. 158; see also p. 75, *ibid* and Add. MSS. 4940.

[23] Add. MSS. 5478.

[24] Add. MSS. 5011.

[25] *S.C.* p. 282.

[26] Add. MSS. 6871. Alexander VI was the Borgia Pope and father of Caesar Borgia. Ximenes was Archbishop of Toledo at the beginning of the sixteenth century and one of the chief Inquisitors.

[27] Add. MSS. 5013.

[28] *H.O.F.* p. 70.

[29] Add. MSS. 5019.

[30] Add. MSS. 6871 and *L.M.G.* p. 83.

[31] *L.M.G.* p. 2.

[32] Add. MSS. 4904.

[33] Add. MSS. 4915.

[34] Add. MSS. 4907.

[35] Add. MSS. 5504.

[36] Add. MSS. 5478.

[37] Add. MSS. 4904.

[38] *L.M.H.* pp. 156 ff.

[39] Add. MSS. 4904.

[40] *H.O.F.* p. 573.

[41] *L.M.G.* p. 148.

[42] *L.M.H.* p. 27.

[43] *H.E.S.* p. 290. 'Conscience' is here used with Acton's usual meaning of the knowledge of morality, located in the individual but not derived from the individual.

[44] *H.O.F.* p. 572.

[45] Add. MSS. 4863. There seems to have been only one occasion when the old intimacy was re-established between Acton and Döllinger. It took place in 1886. Döllinger and Gladstone were staying with Acton at Tegernsee. They went climbing in the mountains nearby. On his return Döllinger felt 'exhausted'. He went to Acton's room and, in Acton's words, 'assured me that in reality he knew what I meant and did not disagree with me.' (*S.C.* p. 193.)

[46] *H.O.F.* pp. 4-5. The italics have been added.

[47] Add. MSS. 5449.

[48] Add. MSS. 4951.

[49] *L.M.G.* p. 180.

[50] *L.M.G.* pp. 180-181.

[51] Add. MSS. 5449.

[52] Add. MSS. 4870.

[53] Add. MSS. 5689.

[54] Add. MSS. 4870.

[55] Add. MSS. 5751; *H.E.S.* p. 176.

[56] Add. MSS. 4943.

[57] Add. MSS. 5467: 'Military organisation begins with the French Revolution. But remember Charles VII. It is the product of a Republic, of nationality, democracy and patriotism imitated by Germany and Russia.'

[58] Add. MSS. 5020. In his copy of *Das Kapital* (Hamburg 1872, 2nd edition, pp. 702-703) Acton has marked passages descriptive of the low standard of living of the English agricultural labourer. Similarly, he notes of Engels, whom he calls 'the best writer of the materialist socialists', that 'he made known the errors and the horrors of our factory system' (Add. MSS. 4981).

[59] *L.F.R.* p. 53.

[60] *L.M.G.* p. 72.

[61] Add. MSS. 5487.

[62] Add. MSS. 5017.

[63] For this very important distinction between the two levels in Acton's thought, see pp. 118-119.

[64] Add. MSS. 5588. *Cf.* also 'The Incas had an exact census, a thing unknown to the Spaniards. It was a system of communistic distribution of land and the most terrible despotism on earth' (Add. MSS. 5487).

[65] *L.M.G.* p. 98: *cf.* also 'The effective distinction between liberty and democracy . . . cannot be too strongly drawn' (*H.O.F.* p. 63).

[66] Add. MSS. 4941.

[67] *H.E.S.* p. 183.

[68] *H.O.F.* p. 11.

[69] *H.O.F.* pp. 64-65. Acton also noted: 'Prussian idea of the state – control opinion by newspapers and the future by the schools' (Add. MSS. 4929).

[70] *H.O.F.* p. 93.

[71] Add. MSS. 5602.

[72] Add. MSS. 5504.

[73] Quoted on p. 27.

[74] *S.C.* p. 54.

[75] Add. MSS. 6871.

[76] Add. MSS. 5608.

[77] Add. MSS. 4948.

[78] Add. MSS. 4917.

[79] *L.M.G.* p. 164; *cf.* also a man 'will not reject Catholicism because the Pope sells licences to sin. He will not reject Democracy because he cannot discover the original contract, or Socialism because it aims at spoiling the rich . . .' (Add. MSS. 4932); or again 'every year some zealous Frenchman exposes the iniquities of the Tudors, hoping to discredit the Church of England; and Taine fancies that to show the horrors of the Revolution is a good argument against Democracy' (*L.M.G.* p. 165).

[80] Add. MSS. 6871. The italics have been added.

[81] Add. MSS. 5509.

[82] Quoted on p. 70.

[83] Add. MSS. 4871.

[84] This was, conversely, the basis of his appreciation of Judaism and Mohammedanism, *e.g.* 'Jews, Moslems have an inspired legislator for politics. We have none. An inspired religious system – an independent political system. It follows that the political action is only gradual, and was slow in being found out and has still to grow' (Add. MSS. 5441).

[85] Add. MSS. 5588.

[86] *L.M.G.* pp. 181-182.

[87] Add. MSS. 5594. Theodore Beza was a sixteenth century Huguenot who taught the duty of the civil authority to repress religious error. He thought heresy worse than murder. (Acton discusses his views, *H.O.F.* p. 146.) Suarez was a sixteenth century Jesuit who taught the duty of tyrannicide in the case of a ruler condemned by the Pope.

[88] Add. MSS. 4944 and 5392.

[89] Add. MSS. 4980. This does not contradict Acton's support for the principle of the separation of Church and State, nor does it make him into a supporter of the theocratic State with its provision for two spheres of authority. As against the first, the claim of the ideal cannot be confused with the benefit of a transient achievement; as against the second, the two sources of authority must be united and the actual conduct of the State

subordinated to the ideal claim. The 'sanctification of Society' demands no less.

[90] Add. MSS. 4868.

[91] Add. MSS. 5392. *Cf.* also: 'Early Christianity – idea that a soldier must serve even in an unjust war' (Add. MSS. 4868).

[92] Add. MSS. 5441.

[93] *H.O.F.* p. 31.

[94] Add. MSS. 5021.

[95] Add. MSS. 5011.

[96] This expression is taken from *H.O.F.* p. 383.

CHAPTER IV

[1] Add. MSS. 4921.

[2] *H.E.S.* pp. 360-362.

[3] *Die Welt als Wille und Vorstellung*, vol. II, chapter 38.

[4] Add. MSS. 5670.

[5] Quoted Add. MSS. 5548. Louis Claude de Saint-Martin (1743-1803) was a French Catholic philosopher who taught a kind of mysticism drawn in part from cabalistic sources. He was much influenced by the German mystic Jacob Boehme.

[6] *H.O.F.* p. 568.

[7] Add. MSS. 4960.

[8] Add. MSS. 4984.

[9] Add. MSS. 5011. The Treaty of Utrecht was signed in 1713. The provision to which Acton is here referring was the cession by Spain to Great Britain of a monopoly for thirty years of the Slave trade with Spanish America (the *Asiento*). The monopoly had been hitherto enjoyed by France. There could be no clearer distinction between Acton's Liberalism and that of the conventional Liberal agnostic than in *this* treatment of Utrecht and that of H. A. L. Fisher. The latter writes: 'The Treaty of Utrecht, based on a wise series of compromises, left behind it no occasion for rancorous dispute' (*History of Europe*, p. 727, 1939 edition).

[10] Add. MSS. 4919.

[11] *L.F.R.* pp. 92-93.

[12] Add. MSS. 5020.

[13] *L.F.R.* p. 92.

[14] This point is further dealt with on pp. 86 ff.

[15] Acton's review of Talleyrand's *Memoirs* is reprinted in

Historical Essays and Studies, pp. 393-413, whence all the above extracts are taken.

[16] Add. MSS. 4982.

[17] Add. MSS. 5011.

[18] *H.O.F.* p. 212. Machiavelli lived from 1469-1527.

[19] Add. MSS. 5449. Another unnamed source, quoted elsewhere in the notes attributes a similar statement to Sir Walter Raleigh: 'Did you ever know of any that were pirates for millions? They only that work for small things are Pirates' (Add. MSS. 4916).

[20] Acton's Introduction to *The Prince*, on which all the foregoing is based, is reprinted in *History of Freedom and Other Essays*, pp. 212-231.

[21] *L.F.R.* p. 300.

[22] Add. MSS. 5449.

[23] *L.M.H.* p. 42.

[24] Add. MSS. 4976.

[25] T. S. Eliot, *The Hollow Men.*

[26] *Weltgeschichtliche Betrachtungen*, chapter I.

CHAPTER V

[1] See p. 37.

[2] Add. MSS. 4981.

[3] Add. MSS. 4987, 5641.

[4] *S.C.* p. 227.

[5] Add. MSS. 4987. Newman called progress 'a slang term' (W. Ward, *The Life of John Henry Cardinal Newman*, vol. II, p. 81, London 1912).

[6] *E.g.* 'Many special ideas of the century [*i.e.* the 18th] only possible by restriction of the Church; Toleration, for the Church persecuted; Humanity, for the Church tortured, and preferred aggravated punishment; Education, for the Church did not encourage it for its own sake, beyond its own influence and sphere; Emancipation, for the Church did not discourage the practice that placed pagan slaves under Christian masters and influences; Freedom of the Press, for the Church promoted Censorship, the Censure and the prohibition and expurgation' (Add. MSS. 4921).

[7] *S.C.* pp. 216-217.

[8] Add. MSS. 5011. There are occasional passages where Acton does indeed speak in glowing terms of the future and of its gradual conquest of the past, as here for example: 'Taking long periods we perceive the advance of moral over material influence, the triumph of general ideas, the gradual amendment. The line of march will prove, on the whole, to have been from force and cruelty to consent and association, to humanity, rational persuasion, and the persistent appeal to common, simple and evident maxims. We have dethroned necessity, in the shape both of hunger and of fear, by extending the scene from Western Europe to the whole world, so that all shall contribute to the treasure of civilisation, and by taking into partnership in the enjoyment of its rewards those who are far off as well as those who are below' (*L.M.H.* p. 33). A proclamation such as this cuts athwart Acton's whole view of history and is ultimately to be explained on psychological grounds. Acton's resolution in not succumbing to illusions was not always equal to the burdens he thereby imposed upon himself. The remarks just quoted are on a par with his extravagant eulogy of the American Revolution (see Appendix).

[9] *L.M.H.* p. 21.

[10] Add. MSS. 4921.

[11] Add. MSS. 5438 and 5594.

[12] Add. MSS. 5588.

[13] Add. MSS. 5002.

[14] Add. MSS. 4986.

[15] *H.O.F.* pp. xxxviii-xxxix.

[16] Add. MSS. 4986.

[17] Add. MSS. 4951.

[18] Add. MSS. 4941.

[19] See above p. 89.

[20] See above p. 88.

[21] *Weltgeschichtliche Betrachtungen*, chapter III.

[22] Add. MSS. 4980.

[23] Add. MSS. 5011, 4960.

[24] Add. MSS. 4906. Acton once noted down the Marxist definition of the culminating point of history: 'From the domain of necessity to the domain of liberty' (quoted Add. MSS. 4960). He makes no comment, but the similarity of view is unmistakable.

[25] Add. MSS. 5020.
[26] Add. MSS. 5615.
[27] *L.F.R.* p. 94.
[28] *Ibid*, p. 93.
[29] Quoted *L.F.R.* p. 92.
[30] *H.E.S.* pp. 182-183.
[31] Add. MSS. 5462, 5467.
[32] *H.E.S.* p. 346.
[33] Add. MSS. 4921.
[34] Add. MSS. 5579.
[35] Add. MSS. 5433. The theme of emotional intrusion into certain of Acton's judgments, with special reference to the American Revolution, is further dealt with in the Appendix.

CHAPTER VI

[1] Add. MSS. 5638.
[2] Add. MSS. 4907.
[3] *L.M.H.* p. 7.
[4] *Ibid*, p. 318. There is a partial qualification to this in that Acton was prepared to allow 'the strongest and most impressive personalities' – he instances Mommsen, Macaulay, Treitschke and Thiers – 'to project their own broad shadow upon their pages'. This he called 'a practice proper to great men, and a great man may be worth several immaculate historians' (*L.M.H.* p. 12). But this viewpoint is isolated amongst the many assertions to the contrary.
[5] *L.F.R.* p. 373.
[6] *Ibid.*
[7] Add. MSS. 5639.
[8] Add. MSS. 4997.
[9] *H.O.F.* p. 221 ('The best touchstone is time').
[10] Add. MSS. 5020.
[11] See above p. 55.
[12] Add. MSS. 4912.
[13] *H.E.S.* p. 355.
[14] *L.M.H.* p. 228.
[15] *L.M.H.* p. 26.
[16] Add. MSS. 4997, 5011.
[17] Add. MSS. 5645, 4909.

[18] *H.E.S.* p. 354.

[19] Max Horkheimer, *The Eclipse of Reason*, New York 1947, p. 182.

[20] *H.O.F.* p. 71.

[21] Add. MSS. 5422.

[22] *H.O.F.* p. 270.

[23] Add. MSS. 6871.

[24] *L.F.R.* p. 372. The italics have been added.

[25] Add. MSS. 5663.

[26] Add. MSS. 4862.

[27] Add. MSS. 5011.

[28] Add. MSS. 4909, 4981.

[29] Add. MSS. 5641.

[30] Add. MSS. 4981, 5011. It is well worth while to compare this view with Nietzche's: 'In order to be able to live, he (*i.e.* man) must have the power, which he must from time to time apply, to destroy and dissolve a past: this he attains by bringing it to judgment, closely scrutinising it and finally condemning it; but every past deserves to be condemned – for that is the way of human affairs: human violence and weakness have always been powerful in them. It is not justice that is here sitting in judgment; still less is it grace which pronounces the verdict: but it is life alone, that dark, driving, inexhaustibly self-desiring force. Its decree is always unkind, always unjust, because it has never flowed from a pure well of knowledge; but in most cases it would speak with the same voice as though justice itself were speaking' (*Vom Nutzen und Nachteil der Historie, Unzeitgemässe Betrachtungen*).

[31] Add. MSS. 5648.

[32] Add. MSS. 4981.

CHAPTER VII

[1] Add. MSS. 5504.

[2] Jacob Burckhardt, *Briefe, Zweiter Teil*, Leipzig 1935, pp. 348-349.

[3] For the substance of the following criticism, acknowledgement is gratefully made to Erich Unger's *The Imagination of Reason*, London 1952.

[4] *H.F.R.* p. 668, April 1863.

[5] Add. MSS. 4993.
[6] Add. MSS. 4940, 5478.
[7] Add. MSS. 4946.
[8] Add. MSS. 4981.
[9] See *e.g.*, Add. MSS. 4940.
[10] Add. MSS. 4865.
[11] *H.O.F.* p. 71.
[12] Add. MSS. 5392.
[13] Book I, *Transcendental Dialectic, Critique of Pure Reason*, Everyman edition, translated, Meiklejohn.

APPENDIX

[1] Mary Drew, *Acton, Gladstone and Others*, p. 2, London 1924.
[2] *H.O.F.* p. 586.
[3] *L.F.R.* p. 34.
[4] Gertrude Himmelfarb, 'The American Revolution in the Theory of Lord Acton', *Journal of Modern History* (Chicago), December 1949.
[5] In the same spirit Acton could pen a note that would do credit to a Torquemada. He would force men to be free: 'Liberalism essentially revolutionary. Facts must yield to ideas. Peaceably and patiently if possible. Violently, if not.... The existence of families and nations not to be balanced against the existence of wrong' (Add. MSS. 5654).

BIBLIOGRAPHY

Abbreviated titles, where used, are given in parentheses after the full title

I: ACTON'S WORKS AND CORRESPONDENCE

History of Freedom and Other Essays, London 1907 (*H.O.F.*).

Historical Essays and Studies, London 1908 (*H.E.S.*).

Lectures on the French Revolution, London 1910 (*L.F.R.*).

Lectures on Modern History, London 1950 (*L.M.H.*).

Sendschreiben an einen deutschen Bischof des Vatikanischen Concils, Nördlingen 1870.

'Quirinus'; *Letters from Rome on the Council*, authorised English translation, London 1870.

Lord Acton and his Circle, edited by Abbot Gasquet, London 1906 (*L.A.C.*).

Letters to Mary Gladstone, edited by Herbert Paul, London 1904 (*L.M.G.*(1)).

Letters to Mary Gladstone, edited by Herbert Paul, London 1913 (*L.M.G.*).

Selections from the Correspondence of the First Lord Acton, edited by Figgis and Lawrence, London 1917 (*S.C.*).

Articles and Reviews in *The Rambler*, *The Home and Foreign Review*, *The Chronicle*, and *The North British Review*.

Add. MSS. in the Cambridge University Library and the British Museum.

II: BIOGRAPHICAL STUDIES AND REFERENCES TO ACTON, ETC.

Auchmuty, James J. *Acton's Election as an Irish Member of Parliament*, English Historical Review, vol. LXI, 1946.

Lady Blennerhassett's article in *Deutsche Rundschau*, January 1905.

Lady Blennerhassett's article in *Edinburgh Review*, April 1903.

Bryce, James. *Studies in Contemporary Biography*, London 1903.

Drew, Mary (*i.e.* Mary Gladstone). *Acton, Gladstone and Others*, London 1924.

Fitzmaurice, Lord Edmond. *Life of the 2nd Earl Granville*, London 1905.

Gibbon, Edward. *Autobiography* (Everyman edition).

Grant Duff, Sir Mountstuart. *Out of the Past*, London 1903.

Life and Letters of Mandell Creighton, by his wife, London 1913.

Maitland, Professor F. W., in *Cambridge Review*, 16th October 1902.

Mathew, Bishop David. *Acton: The Formative Years*, London 1946.

Morley, John Viscount. *Recollections*, London 1924.

Morley, John Viscount. *Life of Gladstone*, London 1912 edition.

Oman, Sir Charles. *On the Writing of History*, London 1939.

III: STUDIES, REVIEWS, ETC, OF ACTON'S WORKS

Brinton, Crane. *Acton's Philosophy of History*, Harvard Theological Review, June 1919.

Brinton, Crane. *English Political Thought in the Nineteenth Century*, London, 2nd edition, 1949.

Butterfield, Herbert. *Lord Acton*, Historical Association Pamphlet, London 1948.

Butterfield, Herbert. *Journal of Lord Acton*, Rome 1857, Cambridge Historical Journal, vol. VIII, No. 3.

Edited and introduced by Douglas Woodruff. *Essays on Church and State*. London 1952.

Fasnacht, G. E. *Acton on Nationality and Socialism*, Oxford 1948.

Fasnacht, G. E. *Acton's Political Philosophy*, London 1952.

Fisher, H. A. L. *Studies in History and Politics*, Oxford 1920.

Gooch, G. P. *History and Historians in the Nineteenth Century*, London 1913.

Gooch, G. P. *Lord Acton: Apostle of Liberty*, Foreign Affairs, July 1947.

Himmelfarb, Gertrude, edited and with an introduction by. *Lord Acton: Essays on Freedom and Power*, Boston 1948 (*F.A.P.*).

Himmelfarb, Gertrude. *The American Revolution in the Political Theory of Lord Acton*, Journal of Modern History (Chicago), vol. XXI, No. 4.

Janossi, Engel de. *The Acton-Creighton Correspondence*, Cambridge Historical Journal, vol. VI, No. 3.

Noack, Ulrich. *Geschichtswissenschaft und Wahrheit: nach den Schriften von John Dalberg-Acton*, Frankfurt 1935.

Noack, Ulrich. *Katholizität und Geistesfreiheit: nach den Schriften von John Dalberg-Acton*, Frankfurt 1936.

Noack, Ulrich. *Politik als Sicherung der Freiheit: nach den Schriften von John Dalberg-Acton*, Frankfurt 1947.

Smith, R. A. L. Article on Acton in New Statesman and Nation, vol. XXVII, No. 692.

Woodward, E. L. *The Place of Lord Acton in the Liberal Movement of the Nineteenth Century*, Politica, September 1939.

IV: OTHER WORKS REFERRED TO

Butterfield, H. *The Whig Interpretation of History*, London 1950.

Burckhardt, Jacob. *Weltgeschichtliche Betrachtungen.*

Burckhardt, Jacob. *Briefe, Zweiter Teil*, Leipzig 1935.

Collingwood, R. G. *The Historical Imagination*, Oxford 1935.

Collingwood, R. G. *The Idea of History*, Oxford 1946.

Fisher, H. A. L. *The History of Europe*, 1947 edition.

Hodges, H. G. *Wilhelm Dilthey – An Introduction*, London 1947.

Kant, Immanuel. *Critique of Pure Reason*, translated by J. M. D. Meiklejohn, Everyman edition.

Lessing, Theodor. *Geschichte als Sinngebung des Sinnlosen*, Munich 1919.

Löwith, Karl. *Meaning in History*, Chicago 1949.

Morgenthau, H. J. *Scientific Man versus Power Politics*, London 1947.

Nietzsche, Friedrich. *Vom Nutzen und Nachteil der Historie für das Leben.*

Ogg, David. *Herbert Fisher*, London 1947.

Schopenhauer, Arthur. *Die Welt als Wille und Vorstellung.*

Shorter, C. K. *Immortal Memories*, London 1907.

Unger, E. *The Imagination of Reason*, London 1952.

Index

INDEX

INDEX